That's
My
Child

Strategies for Parents of
Children with Disabilities

Lizanne Capper

Child & Family Press

Washington, DC

Child & Family Press
an imprint of the Child Welfare League of America, Inc.

CHILD WELFARE LEAGUE OF AMERICA, INC.
440 First Street, NW, Suite 310, Washington, DC 20001-2085

CURRENT PRINTING (last digit)
10 9 8 7 6 5 4 3 2

Cover design by Paul Butler
Text design by Eve Malakoff-Klein and Jennifer M. Price

Printed in the United States of America

Library of Congress Cataloging-in-Publication Data
Capper, Lizanne.
    That's my child : strategies for parents of children with disabilities / Lizanne Capper.
        p.   cm.
    Includes bibliographical references and index.
    ISBN # 0-87868-595-2   (pbk.)
    1. Parents of handicapped children--United States.   2. Handi-capped
children--Services for--United States.   I. Title.
HQ759.913.C36   1996
362.4'083--dc20   95-36682

I dedicate this book to my daughter, Lara,
for whom I wish happiness and independence.
I would also like to thank all the people who helped
with this book, especially my friend, Cyndy Taymore,
and my sister and dear friend, Jean Capper.
You both provided gracious encouragement
and sound advice.

Contents

Introduction

I am the mother of a child with disabilities. It is the most challenging job I have ever undertaken and the most rewarding. Throughout the years since it was determined that my daughter has a language-based learning disability and Attention Deficit Disorder (ADD), I have struggled to get the best services for her and for me. The struggle has been both frustrating and gratifying. I have learned about the education laws, the school systems, my daughter's disabilities, other disabilities, human nature, and myself. In this book, I share the experiences of parents of children with disabilities and of the people who support them in their search to get the best and to be the best for their children.

Most parents work to help their children learn, but those whose children have disabilities find the work can be harder and filled with many challenges. To help our children we often must acquire knowledge through experience and from teachers, doctors, other parents, our children, and countless others. We must teach ourselves so that we may teach our children. The search for knowledge and support is sometimes difficult.

The disabling conditions that have come to be called special needs can range from a mild hearing loss to profound mental retardation. Whatever the disability, the parents of children with disabilities are often looking for the same thing—support.

In this book, we will explore the different sources of support available to you as the parent of a child with disabilities.

Although parents are the primary audience for this book, it is my hope that the members of support networks and others will find this book useful. To ensure that children with disabilities reach their full potential, people in support networks must empathize with parents. They must understand how our children are different and how this affects our lives. They must appreciate the anguish with which most of us have accepted these differences. Most of all, people who assist the parents of children with disabilities and in turn help these children, must be compassionate. And all of us, when dealing with our special children, must focus on what our children *can* do rather than on what they cannot do.

Whatever your child's disability may be, your family is not alone. There are approximately 43 million people with disabilities in the United States. The federal Individuals with Disabilities Education Act (IDEA) governs all state special education laws and regulations. Most state regulations include definitions of the following handicapping conditions: autism, deafness, hearing impairment, visual handicap, mental retardation, orthopedic impairment, other health impairments such as cerebral palsy, serious emotional disturbance, specific learning disabilities, and preschool developmental delay. ADD is also considered a disability when it can be shown to adversely affect a child's school performance.

Many resources are available to you and your child. As we look for answers from these resources, we find more questions. The search can seem endless—in many ways it is like an occupation—but it is an important search because you must work to get the right services for your child. You must learn about the law, your child's disability, teaching methods, and your child's unique needs. With this knowledge will come confidence, and with confidence you will be able to be a strong advocate for your child. You may have to play the role of advocate throughout your child's life. If you are fortunate, your awareness and self-assurance will enable your child to self-advocate as he or she grows older.

Throughout your child's life you are likely to dwell from time to time on the reasons for your child's disability. Although there are known causes for many disabilities, many remain mysteries. Parents often agonize over this and spend much time and money trying to find an answer. As hard as it may be to accept, the best thing we can do for our children is to love them for who they are and make sure they have opportunities for growth and independence.

To help our children reach their potential, we must reach out to our support network. This network includes a formal component (school systems, physicians, therapists, and support organizations) and an informal component (other parents of children with disabilities, friends, family, and others). We all have our own needs based upon our background, personality, and our child's disability. But we share one thing in common: we want the best for our children.

In the chapters that follow, we will explore the resources available to you and your child. We will discover what a support network is, what services it can provide, and how to make it work for your family. Parents of children with disabilities want strategies that work. As one mother of a child with ADD said,

"I want a behavior management program, not a theory. I want to know what to do."

In later chapters, you'll learn some approaches for working with your child, as well as some practical ideas for developing and maintaining good relationships with the other people in your child's life. We will also explore two persons who may not come to mind when you think of your support network: yourself and your child. Working with a child who has a disability requires a team effort and you and your child are critical members of that team.

The book is divided into chapters associated with different aspects of support networks. One chapter is also dedicated to the laws affecting persons with disabilities. Books and resources referred to throughout the text are listed in the appendixes, along with information on additional resources and support organizations.

This book cannot answer all of your questions. Rather, it is intended to provide guidance as you look for places to find answers. It is my hope that it will not only lead you to the right places for answers, but also to accept the fact that for some questions, there are no answers.

A disability not only challenges your child, but also tests your family's patience, your confidence, your trust in others, your marriage, and at times even your sanity. The most important thing to remember is that you know your child best and you have the opportunity to make the greatest impact on his or her life. With a commitment to learning for you and your child, your family can face the challenges and—with love, understanding, perseverance, and support—overcome them.

Building a network and team for your child with disabilities can be hard work. You cannot rest on your laurels for long, because as your child grows older your support team must change in size and makeup. Your work with others, however, is critical to your child's potential for growth, independence, and happiness, and to the future he or she deserves.

* * *

I have mentioned the names of many who have helped me or otherwise played an important part in the experience on which this book is based. Many consented to the use of their names. A diamond (◆) following a name indicates that it has been changed.

1 The One Who Will Always Be There—You

If someone asked you to define your support network, you might not think of yourself. Perhaps because I am a single parent and live 900 miles from my family, I have come to view myself as my most important source of support. Even if you have a supportive spouse and family close by, however, being able to rely on yourself can provide you with a sense of security. This confidence can ease the pain of losing part of your support network, possibly as the result of a move, death, or divorce. Being an advocate for your child allows you to draw upon your knowledge to support yourself in times of need and in times of despair. It gives you a great sense of empowerment when dealing with professionals and can make you feel good about yourself. Most importantly, it enables you to be a champion for your child.

Accepting the Difference

Some parents are hit all at once with the reality that their child has a disability. Others find out gradually. Whether you knew that your child had a disability when he or she was ten hours old or ten years old, accepting it can be hard. Over the years in which the various diagnoses were made for my daughter, I went through a myriad of emotions. I felt anguish, guilt, anger, depression, anxiety, embarrassment, denial, grief, and hopelessness. I felt overwhelmed. I also hid from the truth, being overly pessimistic one day and overly optimistic the next. What kept me going through this period was my determination to learn everything I could about Lara's disabilities and to make sure that she was receiving the right treatment and services. Being actively involved in my local special education parent advisory council also helped a great deal. Sharing my knowledge with other parents, as well as learning from them, have been good sources of support.

Most parents of children with disabilities want answers. They are unsettled by their inability to know what the future holds for their child. One mother of an eight-year-old with Turner's syndrome* wants desperately to know what the quality of her daughter's life will be. Unfortunately, there is no crystal ball. With certain disabilities a specific prognosis can be made, but with many disabilities, professionals working with your child can give only a general picture of what the future will bring.

Acceptance will come to you in several stages. One is accepting that something is wrong—that something about your child is different. Another is accepting that having a child with a disability means a different life for your child than you had hoped for—and a different life for you. You have to work harder to be a good parent to such a child. You have to know more about the law, educational options, medicine, and your child. You also have to be more patient and play more roles than the parent of a "normal" child.

For some parents, accepting their child's disability is easy.

A psychologist's daughter was having trouble at college and diagnosed herself as having ADD. Once formally diagnosed and taking medication, Susan,♦ a very bright 19-year-old, excelled at school. Accepting Susan's disability was relatively easy for her family because she was able to quickly compensate.

---

* Turner's syndrome is a chromosomal abnormality in which a girl has only one X chromosome.

♦ A diamond following a name indicates that the name has been changed.

Parents of children with severe disabilities have a particularly difficult task ahead of them. Children with physical disabilities or antisocial behavior such as autism may find it difficult to share affection. It may be hard if not impossible to hold and nurture these children. As eloquently described in Helen Featherstone's *A Difference in the Family: Living with a Disabled Child*, acceptance can be a lifelong affair.

Each individual has his or her own way of dealing with adversity—some more effective than others. Most parents of children with a disability find it liberating to reach the point of acceptance. For years I kept my daughter's disabilities private at work. When I announced my decision to leave my job to write this book, I reached a new level of acceptance of Lara. Talking openly about Lara with my co-workers reinforced my faith in others for their ability to accept differences. It was okay for me to have a unique and special child, and my experience as Lara's mother has made me a more interesting and compassionate person.

Talking with others can provide valuable support. Many parents who have children with disabilities draw support from each other. By sharing experiences and strategies, you learn effective coping techniques, educate yourself, and educate others. It can also be rewarding to discuss your child's disability and its impact on your life with family, friends, and even acquaintances. You will get a good deal of advice you should disregard, but you will also get ideas that may work.

Regardless of the nature of your child's disability, you must put aside the mental picture of your child that you created before he or she was born and accept your child for who he or she is. This movement from dreams to reality may take weeks or even years. You may be pulled back into the acceptance process from time to time, such as when a new diagnosis is made or when your child experiences a setback. As one father put it,

Know that moments of discouragement are going to come and it's normal to feel that way. You can't really completely avoid it. It's going to happen and your success as

a parent is directly related to your ability to deal with that. You're going to have rough times. And you're not unusual because you're having rough times. You're not a failure because you have rough times.

Many parents find that focusing on their child's positive qualities pulls them through these rough times. Playing all the roles of a parent can also make you too busy to dwell on the negative!

The Roles You Play

As a parent, you play many roles—chauffeur, nurse, social worker, and more. For most children, parents are the most important persons in their lives. Children depend on parents for food, clothing, shelter, guidance, and love. For children with disabilities, dependence on parents is greater than for typical children. The roles we play are often the same as we would play for other children, but the intensity is affected by the needs of our children. As a parent, you will feel that dependence as you advocate for your child and promote his or her positive self-esteem and independence. We are our children's champions.

Parents have the opportunity, and therefore the responsibility, to know their children best. *You* are the expert on your child. Like any expert, you need to have a solid understanding of all child care disciplines so that you can communicate and work effectively with the people providing services for your child. Being an expert will give you confidence in dealing with other experts who work with your child. It will also give you the conviction to trust your instincts when you believe one thing and professionals tell you another.

The perfect parent does not exist. We all make mistakes in the roles we play. We learn from our mistakes, and so do our children. Simply wanting your child to reach his or her potential and to be happy goes a long way in ensuring the achievement of your goal. And love goes a long, long way in making all persons feel good about themselves.

The Role of Advocate

To be a good advocate, you must know the law, the process, and the people. Good advocates are also assertive. As you will discover in Chapter 5 on rights and services under federal law, law and process go hand in hand. Knowledge of federal, state, and local regulations and procedures allows you to concentrate on the most important issue: getting the right services for your child.

Negotiating for and assisting in the delivery of services for your child requires contact with many people. Knowing who these people are and what they can do for your child builds better working relationships. But the most important person for you to know is your child.

Being aware of your child's strengths and weaknesses is critical to being his or her advocate. I have found it helpful to develop a profile of my daughter, listing her strengths as well as her weaknesses. (The next few pages provide a sample.) In *The Misunderstood Child*, Dr. Larry Silver proposes a good method for developing profiles of children with learning disabilities. The definition of your child's disability can also be a guide in this process.* Do not forget about strengths in your child's personality, such as cheerfulness, compassion, or assertiveness. Although it is important to understand your child's weaknesses, it is equally important to emphasize the positive.

Having a comprehensive picture of your child will help you work with the professionals in your child's life. Share a copy of the profile of your child with those who work with him or her. Ask others to offer their thoughts and opinions. Developing or re-reading the profile of your child can also help you to put things into perspective and remind you of your child's strengths and positive attributes.

Although not knowing the cause of your child's disability can be overwhelming and hard to accept, your primary focus should be on treatment. Treatment may come in the form of

---

* Definitions for several disabilities may be found in Appendix A.

A Profile of Lara

General

Lara is a happy, loving girl. She has a cute personality and often makes those around her laugh. She talks nonstop out of school, chattering about events and feelings. She is quite organized and takes responsibility for the neatness of her room and of our basement. Lara enjoys school and socializing with friends and family. She loves life!

Specific Learning Disabilities

[Areas of Ability (*A*) and of Disability (*D*)]

I. Input Disabilities

    A. *Visual Perception (Processing) Disabilities*
    A person with a <u>Visual Perception Disability</u> has difficulty with one or more of the following:

A	1.	spatial positioning
D	2.	organizing self in space/distinguishing between left and right
A	3.	figure versus background focus
A	4.	judging distance
A	5.	eye-hand coordination

    B. *Auditory Perception (Processing) Disabilities (difficulty understanding language)*
    A person with an <u>Auditory Perception Disability</u> has difficulty with one or more of the following:

D	1.	distinguishing subtle differences in sounds
D	2.	figure versus background focus
D	3.	auditory lag

continued...

II.   Integration Disabilities (Conceptualization difficulties)
A person with an Integration Disability has one or more of the following difficulties in putting pieces together into a meaningful whole and understanding basic ideas.

   A.   *Sequencing*
     <u>A</u>   1.   with visual inputs
     <u>D</u>   2.   with auditory inputs

   B.   *Abstraction*
     <u>D</u>   1.   with visual inputs
     <u>D</u>   2.   with auditory inputs

III. Memory Disabilities
A person with a Memory Disability has difficulty with one or more of the following:

   A.   *Short-term memory*
     <u>D</u>   1.   with visual inputs
     <u>D</u>   2.   with auditory inputs

   B.   *Long-term memory*
     <u>A</u>   1.   with visual inputs
     <u>A</u>   2.   with auditory inputs

IV. Output Disabilities (Expression difficulties)
A person with an Output Disability has difficulty with one or more of the following:

   A.   <u>*Expressive language*</u>
     <u>D</u>   1.   demand language
     <u>D</u>   2.   spontaneous language

   B.   <u>*Motor functioning*</u>
     <u>D</u>* 1.   gross motor
     <u>A</u>   2.   fine motor

---

* Although Lara has difficulty with gross motor planning, this is an area of relative strength.

continued...

Characteristics of ADD

(<u>Y</u> = applies to Lara, <u>N</u> = does not apply to Lara)

Y 1. often fidgets with hands or feet or squirms in seat (in adolescence may be limited to subjective feelings of restlessness)

Y 2. has difficulty remaining seated when required to do so

Y 3. is easily distracted by extraneous stimuli

N 4. has difficulty awaiting turns in games or group situations

N 5. often blurts out answers to questions before they have been completed

Y 6. has difficulty following through on instructions from others (not due to oppositional behavior or failure of comprehension)

Y 7. has difficulty sustaining attention in tasks or play activities

Y 8. often shifts from one uncompleted activity to another

N 9. has difficulty playing quietly

Y 10. often talks excessively

N 11. often interrupts or intrudes on others, e.g. butts into other children's games

Y 12. often does not seem to listen to what is being said to him or her

N 13. often loses things necessary for tasks or activities at school or at home

N 14. often engages in physically dangerous activities without considering possible consequences (not for the purpose of thrill-seeking), e.g., runs into street without looking— Lara *sometimes* crosses the street without first looking both ways

continued...

Language Disorders

(many overlap with Learning Disabilities)
(*Y* = applies to Lara, *N* = does not apply to Lara)

I. Semantic

    (trouble understanding the "meaning" of language)

    N   A.   comprehension (might have trouble learning colors, names of common objects, and adjective pairs)

    Y *   B.   expression (word-finding problems)

II. Syntactic

    Y *   A.   comprehension (immature understanding of sentences)

    Y *   B.   expression (trouble using sentences to communicate)

III. Pragmatic

    (how to use language to interact with others—has difficulty understanding the rules that govern the use of language in social situations)

    Y   A.   comprehension

    N   B.   expression

IV. Discourse

    (how to organize sentences into a conversation, such as stories)

    Y *   A.   comprehension

    Y *   B.   expression

---

* We have seen great improvement in this area this past year or so.

special education services, medical treatment, psychotherapy, behavior management, and so on. Many parents also find that planning for their child's future is beneficial, both to their child and to themselves.

> *Cyndy and Jack, parents of a 14-year-old with language-based learning disabilities, developed three plans for their son. One is for the next year, another covers the next five years, and the last contains goals for when he turns 22.*

These plans can serve as excellent tools to help you communicate with the professionals working with your child. (A sample plan for the future appears on the next page.)

Selecting two or three goals to concentrate on at a time has been effective in promoting my daughter's development. She and I select from the general categories of academic goals, behavior improvement goals, and basic living-skills acquisition. For example, at age nine, Lara's goals were (1) read four books a week (academic), (2) ask for dessert only when she has finished her meal (behavior), and (3) learn the sequence of the months to the point where she can, given a month, name the preceding and following months (basic living). We keep track of the books she reads on her calendar (which also reinforces our work on learning the names and sequence of the months), and she will earn the doll of her choice when she accomplishes her weekly goal for six weeks in a row. We also have mutually agreed upon time frames and rewards for the other two goals.

These goals allowed Lara to address several areas affected by her disabilities. Her learning disabilities make reading a challenge. She also has sequencing problems, which make it difficult for her to comprehend time. Her Attention Deficit Disorder makes her impulsive and perseverative, and having reinforcement to think before she asks for dessert gave her the edge to overcome this behavior problem.

Developing even a one-year plan for your child helps you put things into perspective and to have realistic expectations about your child's future. Though it may remind you of your child's limitations, it also reinforces your child's abilities. Looking ahead to adulthood helps keep a balance in the relationship

A Plan for Lara's Future
Lara in Third Grade

(See the attached documentation for a description of Lara's annual home goals and objectives, learning style, strengths, and weaknesses.)

I believe Lara can be integrated into the third grade more so than in past years. I think two of her inclusion objectives should be:

1) Lara will actively participate in general classroom discussion, progressing beyond active listening and attentiveness (which she achieved in second grade) to contributing personal experiences and opinions.

2) Lara will complete academic assignments from the special education teacher in the general classroom at least once per week in the fall, twice per week in the winter, and thrice per week in the spring.

Lara in Five Years

Lara will be 14 years old in five years (which seems hard to believe!). I envision Lara to be doing well socially, probably with a boyfriend (oh, my!). I believe Lara will have accomplished all basic living skills (with the likely exception of cooking). In other words, she will be able to understand the concept of time and manage money, skills upon which she is now working. (She has obtained most other basic living skills at this time, including caring for her clothes (she helps with laundry and puts her clothes away regularly), keeping her room and the basement clean, setting and clearing the table, basic (very basic) cooking, and self-care (selecting outfits, dressing, bathing, hair).

I imagine Lara at the middle school in seventh grade included in a team, receiving academic assistance from a special education teacher and language therapy from a speech and language pathologist. Lara may also participate in a peer group similar to the one she now participates in, but for teens, to develop and refine her social problem solving skills.

Lara at Age 22

I expect Lara to graduate from either a two-year community college with special education services, possibly after three years (thus putting her at 21 or 22) or from a program such as Threshold at Lesley College. She should be able to hold down a job, I imagine as a day care teacher, and live independently. Lara is friendly, cute, and compassionate. I imagine that she will marry and may have children of her own.

between things that seem so important while a child is in school and what adulthood calls for.

> *Mary,*◆ *the mother of a child with a learning disability and ADD, was reminded by a friend that her daughter is not likely to need algebra after she graduates from high school.*

If your child's handwriting is sloppy, just remember the quality of your doctor's signature! Realize that behavior that is annoying now, such as stubbornness, may serve your child very well in adulthood when he or she is advocating for his or her own rights.

Promoting Positive Self-Esteem

When I was a child my ski coach used to say, "Think positive, think positive! Visualize winning!" I try to apply this approach to parenting. As Dr. Silver proposes, "Building on strengths to overcome weaknesses" is the key to the future of a child with a disability. Parents would be negligent if they did not acknowledge weaknesses in their child. To be truly successful, however, a person must have a positive self-image. A positive self-image comes from success and from feeling good about your abilities and knowing that your strengths will enable you to compensate for your weaknesses.

Communication is difficult for even the most articulate, intelligent people because it is a two-way street. It involves gross motor functioning, word retrieval, listening, the ability to relate cause and effect, and many more skills. According to Drs. Mark Batshaw and Ken Bleile in *Your Child Has A Disability*, communication is probably the most difficult activity a person performs.

Many children with disabilities have difficulty with socialization. At one extreme is the autistic child, but a child with even a mild learning disability may also have trouble communicating with peers and family. In *Succeeding Against the Odds*, Sally Smith describes teaching your child the "fourth R"—relationship skills—as one of your most important roles as a parent.

Socialization skills include the ability to communicate as

well as to understand the appropriate actions to take under certain circumstances. The skills require a certain level of common interest with others. Some children with disabilities have great socialization skills. If your child has trouble with these skills, however, you can be a positive influence by using behavior management techniques and by providing examples of appropriate social interaction (and by demonstrating inappropriate examples and then discussing them with your child!). One father and his son write and act out plays together in which they solve socialization and relationship problems. Playing puppets or "producing" puppet shows can also be an effective way of practicing good social skills. *Puppetry for Mentally Handicapped People*, by Caroline Astell-Burt, includes ideas for helping your child develop decision-making and communication skills. Clinics and schools also have programs for developing and maintaining good peer relations. Although helping your child develop socialization skills can be a task with a long and indefinite perspective, it is crucial to his or her well-being.

Fostering Independence

The state of independence you desire for your child will depend on the nature and severity of your child's disability. At one end of the spectrum is the young adult who begins self-advocacy while in high school. At the other end is the severely disabled young adult who accomplishes basic self-help activities.

Self-advocacy skills have to be taught. Involving your child in school meetings, developing plans together, and solving problems together can move your child forward on the path to independence. Educational consultants are available who specialize in teaching self-advocacy skills to adolescents and young adults. Getting your child involved in self-advocacy will relieve some of the pressure on you as well as guide your child toward independence. As one learning disabled college student put it:

Once I started advocating for myself, I realized how hard my parents worked for me. It really made me respect them.

Children with moderate to severe disabilities also need extra assistance in developing self-help and independent living skills. Your child's educational program may be based largely on the development of these skills. *Steps to Independence*, by Drs. Bruce Baker and Alan Brightman, is a good resource for ideas and techniques for working on skills "necessary for getting along in the world." Although geared to children with moderate to severe disabilities, it offers excellent strategies for dealing with tasks confronting all children (get-ready skills, for example). Setting life-skills goals and objectives can be critical if your child has moderate to severe disabilities. Focusing on real-world skills will further your child's move toward independence. Learning to manage money, use the phone, care for possessions, and take public transportation are examples of life-skills goals. Using a system that tracks and rewards progress will help ensure success. Involve your child in making a chart filled with colors and pictures to illustrate improvement.

As described later in Chapter 5, several different independent living options are available for individuals with disabilities. These arrangements may vary as to the level of independence they require. Some programs are for young adults of below- or low-average intelligence; others are for more needy individuals. Planning early in your child's teenage years can make the transition to independence easier for everyone.

Your Independence and Self-Esteem

You may ask yourself, "When do I get time for me?" It is important for your own self-esteem and happiness to carve out time and energy for yourself. If you devote all of yourself to your child's needs, yours will be ignored.

> *Jo Ann realized one day that she did not have to be the mother of a child with Down syndrome 100% of the time; it was healthy for her take time out from her role as mother.*

Having some time away from your child, either alone or with your spouse or a friend, is good for you *and* for your child. You will return refreshed, reenergized, and relaxed. Your child will learn that if you go away, you will return and that other people also have needs. It may help to set goals for yourself, such as having a night out alone with friends once a month.

Working with Professionals

Depending on the severity of your child's disability, you may work with one or many professionals. Although we will discuss effective means of working with specific professionals in later chapters, this section presents some ideas for pulling it all together.

> *One parent keeps a list of all the professionals who work with her daughter. It contains names, areas of expertise, and phone numbers. Another mother, whose child sees eight different doctors and medical professionals periodically, keeps a schedule of the name, type of professional, date of last visit, and date of next visit. This keeps her appointments straight and reminds her when appointments are to be scheduled. This mother also shares this schedule with her ex-husband to facilitate communication.*

Many parents find it helps to keep a file of their child's records. I include everything written about my daughter, including her Individualized Education Plans (IEP), evaluation assessments, medical reports, and my own written plans. I try to keep it sorted in an order that is logical to me, although I change my mind on what is logical from time to time and completely reorganize the drawer! Maintaining a log of the contents of the file makes it easy to locate particular records. Your file can also be compared against school files to make sure that your file contains all the school's records.

I remember being overwhelmed each time I met a new type of professional. They each have a language all their own. I quickly learned that if I wanted to communicate effectively with them, I had to learn their jargon. One father developed his own glossary of terms, which has grown over the years since his son's diagnosis of Down syndrome. Several glossary books are available, such as *A Glossary of Special Education*, by Phillip Williams. If someone is working with your child and you do not understand what is being said, ask him or her to rephrase it. Do not be intimidated to the point where you walk out of an appointment more confused than when you walked in. Keep a running list of questions to bring to appointments. Be assertive—no one can be as concerned for your child as you can. Ask, ask, ask!

Dealing with Strangers

Because our children with disabilities are different, we tend to be more sensitive to the remarks of others. In some instances, strangers may be sincerely interested and simply naive. In other instances, they may be naive but also nasty, making inappropriate comments about a child's appearance or speech. In these latter circumstances it is probably best to give the person a dirty look and walk away. If others ask questions because they are curious and you feel comfortable responding, try to educate them about your child's disability. The more people are educated, the better chance people with disabilities have of being accepted.

Working with Your Child

In promoting independence and your child's self-esteem, it may help to think of yourself as a coach—someone who teaches, guides, pushes, encourages, and cheers. The coach shares in the agony of defeat and rejoices in the thrill of victory. Coaches and their players strategize together and work toward the same goal.

People generally capitalize on their strengths to overcome their weaknesses. They compensate. For most people, this comes naturally. People with disabilities have to learn compensating techniques. For example, a blind person's other senses do not become stronger by themselves. A blind child must be taught to have a heightened sense of hearing, touch, and smell.

To teach our children compensating techniques, it is important to know our own strengths and weaknesses as well as theirs.

You may find it helpful to develop a profile of yourself. Comparing your profile to your child's can highlight areas where you may be of particular help. Being in touch with your own strengths and limitations allows you to draw upon the ways you have compensated.

Transitions are often difficult for children with disabilities, particularly autistic children and children with ADD. Whenever possible, your child should know about plans ahead of time. For example, give your child a two-minute warning before you ask him or her to stop doing one thing and to do another. At some level, we all have trouble moving from one activity to another; particularly when we must stop doing something we like to do something we do not like. When your child frustrates you by refusing to stop playing video games when you've asked him or her to set the table, remember some transition that was difficult for you. Describing to your child how you coped shows that you empathize; it may also give your child the ability to make transitions more easily.

Children with disabilities often have poor organizational skills and weak short-term memories. They may also be distractible. Using lists (if your child cannot read, use pictures instead) can help keep your child on task and better organized. Also, using bright colors to organize your child's room or notebook can help in the development of better organizational skills. For some children, organizational skills are a strength. If this is the case with your child, encourage the use of these organizational abilities to solve problems and compensate for weaknesses. The use of lists is likely to come automatically to such children. They thrive on lists and develop other reminder techniques on their own.

In some cases, children with disabilities can draw upon their social interaction skills as a strength. In many cases, however, they cannot. Blind children often have to be taught appropriate socialization and conversational skills. Autistic children, by definition, have to be taught social interaction and communication skills. Learning disabled and ADD children also often have difficulty interacting with peers and maintaining friendships. In some cases you may be your child's only friend, and you may have to encourage friendships between your child and his or her peers. Betty Osman's book, *No One to Play With: The Social Side to Learning Disabilities*, gives some good suggestions. As your child grows older, his or her friends can reinforce good social skills and dissuade your child from using inappropriate skills. My daughter's friend Jessica is at times far more effective at coaching Lara than I am because Lara will listen to Jess!

Understanding how to read others' emotions and responses can make the difference between communication and miscommunication. An effective technique for teaching children about emotions is to look through a family photo album or magazine and discuss with your child what the different facial expressions suggest.*

Talking with your child will improve his or her vocabulary, communication, and socialization skills. If your child is blind, explain what you are doing. Explain what things look like in understandable terms. Explain the color red by having your child touch something warm, and the color blue by touching something cool, as in the movie "Mask."

Working with your child can be a frustrating experience. You may go for days, weeks—maybe months—without seeing a noticeable difference. Taking a time-out from the day-to-day responsibilities can give you a fresh perspective. Every time I develop new goals and objectives for my daughter, I am reminded of how far she has come since the last time we went through the exercise. It is easy to lose sight of the long term when you are rushing around in the morning getting your children ready for school and yourself ready for work, and the dog is barking and the telephone is ringing. Sometimes growth comes in spurts, and you notice development virtually right in front of your eyes. Usually it comes about more gradually. But when it comes, it is confirmation that your child is progressing—and in large part because of you.

---

* Studying family pictures can also help your child learn the names of infrequently seen relatives. Several games are available to teach children about emotions. (These are available through the ADD Warehouse, listed in Appendix C.)

2 Co-Parents

What is a co-parent? It is the person or persons who have an opportunity to nurture your child and to plan for and have an impact on his or her future. I have chosen to use this term instead of spouse because it is more inclusive. There is a higher incidence of divorce in families with children with disabilities, and you may no longer be married to your child's other biological parent. You may have more than one co-parent. If either you or your ex-spouse have remarried or are living with someone, there may be three or four co-parents. All of these persons are involved to some extent in your child's life.

Common Problems

It is often said that parenthood puts more strain on a marriage than any other condition or event. This stress is compounded when a child has a disability. Your daily reality is likely to be different from the dreams you shared for your marriage.

Raising a child with a disability can accentuate differences in styles between parents. It is important to acknowledge your differences and realize that neither of you is always going to be right. You may be at a different stage of acceptance of your child's disability than your child's other parent. This can cause

19

frustration and sometimes anger in the parent who has more readily accepted the child's situation. You may be more familiar with disabilities than your co-parent. Parents often disagree on treatment, particularly when behavior management is involved. Consistency is important in managing the behavior of a child with disabilities. It may be difficult to sustain that consistency, however, if you do not eye-to-eye with your co-parent.

Sometimes, being in different stages of acceptance is a positive thing:

> *Marcy and Ben describe their marriage as truly supportive because when one of them is down, the other is up and able to pump up the other. Cindy describes her relationship with her husband Tom as a team and a partnership. They work together for their children.*

Although I acknowledged Lara's disabilities from the beginning, I have gone through periods of denial. This is not uncommon. There are cases when one co-parent refuses to accept that there is something wrong. Encouraging your co-parent to speak with professionals or read literature about your child's disability can help him or her move toward acceptance.

> *Betsy,♦ the mother of a daughter recently diagnosed as having learning disabilities, described her husband as not ready to accept fully the diagnosis. Betsy was willing to give her husband time to adjust. In the meantime, however, she had jumped in with both feet and was learning everything she could to help her daughter.*

Parents may blame each other for causing the disability. This is more likely to happen when no cause is known. Talking about your emotions, your dashed hopes, and your resulting fears can dispel some of the blame. On the other hand, suppressing your anger and resentment can lead to poor communication and misunderstanding. Make sure you listen to each other. You and your co-parent are most likely experiencing similar feelings. Sharing your feelings with your co-parent can relieve some of the tension and allow you to work as partners.

It is normal to have awful thoughts. You or your co-parent may wish your child had never been born. Parents of children with severe disabilities may feel torn between their desire for the freedom that would come with a residential placement of their child versus their sense of responsibility for keeping the child at home. You may feel cheated—that you got the wrong baby. These feelings usually come and go, fading over time.

Even if these thoughts have never crossed your mind, they may have crossed your co-parent's mind. Talking openly about them will build a stronger relationship between the two of you. You may wonder how you could even broach the subject.

One father of a child who was severely mentally retarded simply asked his wife one night, "Have you ever thought about David♦ dying?" This one question unlocked the door to discussions between David's parents on other topics they had kept inside themselves for several years.

Working Together as Partners

Whether you are married or not, you and your co-parent are jointly responsible for your child's care. It is likely that one parent shoulders more of the responsibility, particularly for day-to-day activities. Whenever possible, though, you should share responsibilities. If your child requires frequent visits to physicians or therapists, sharing the task distributes the load. If there are team meetings and conferences to attend, do so together. Unfortunately, fathers are less likely to be involved in their child's education, but as my ex-husband says:

Fathers have a critical role. They have to struggle against the temptation to get frustrated and allow themselves to slip out of the loop. They must press on.

If both parents are not able to attend a meeting, planning the agenda together beforehand and discussing the meeting afterward ensures participation by both parents. One mother tapes sessions that her husband is unable to attend.

Planning

Planning for your child's future calls for you and your co-parent to work together. As described in Chapter 1, many parents and professionals recommend developing three plans for a child with disabilities, each with different time horizons. (An example appears on page 11.)

Looking ahead for one year can help you and your co-parent to agree on specific goals and objectives. Working together on a five-year plan compels you to balance your dreams with reality. (Be prepared for disagreements.) You may argue about the goals you want your child to accomplish, as well as the best way to make sure that your child reaches those goals. Finally, focusing on adulthood together helps you and your co-parent in several ways. If you expect that your child will attend college, there are obvious advantages to doing some financial planning. If, however, your child may be financially dependent throughout his or her life, the importance of financial planning cannot be minimized. You and your co-parent may want to seek the advice of a lawyer to ensure that your wills are set up appropriately.

Discussing what your child will be like in adulthood may require you to do some planning for your own lives as well. Although you may not make the decision until many years later, openly discussing the advantages and disadvantages of your child living at home versus some sort of independent living arrangement can be liberating.

Marcy and Ben, parents of a son with epilepsy, ADD, and learning disabilities, began discussing this question when Jacob was seven years old; they have found that it helps keep communication open between them.

Lastly, planning for adulthood gives you an opportunity to look beyond school, which is often a difficult time for children with disabilities. As a psychologist pointed out at a workshop, childhood is merely an obstacle to a normal adulthood for many children. If this is the case for your child, thinking of your child at age 22 can be reassuring.

Making Time for Planning

My ex-husband and I get together periodically for planning sessions for Lara. Bob♦ and Elizabeth,♦ parents of a boy with brain damage, conduct annual planning sessions. Some parents find it beneficial to tie their planning cycle in with the IEP (individualized education plan) development cycle. If you decide to do your planning in conjunction with the IEP, set aside enough time to be sure that your plans are comprehensive and that you have a clear agenda for the IEP meeting.

Ideally, both parents will spend some time preparing on their own before a planning meeting. It is a less ideal but still valuable alternative for one parent to do the preparation. If you cannot engage your co-parent in any sort of planning, do it yourself. Share the results with your co-parent. Some parents have to ease into this process.

Some suggested steps in the planning process are shown on the following pages. You may want to add some of these ideas to your current process or, if you have not yet developed a plan for your child, use these suggestions as a starting point. The planning process may take as long as three to four weeks. Agree with your co-parent on when and how you will develop your plans. You may want to include your child for whom you are planning and your other children in part or all of the planning process. The second time you develop a plan is likely to be different from the first; it will most certainly be easier! You will find that some things that were important one year are irrelevant the next. Over time, the planning process will evolve.

The Impact of Divorce

Divorce is often devastating to family members. For children with disabilities, their parents' divorce may be especially confusing because they may not have the intellectual maturity to understand what has happened, or they may not have the language to fully express their feelings.

My intent is not to dwell on the emotional turmoil caused by divorce, but to acknowledge that it exists.* As a parent, you need to know how to move on and how to work as a team.

Although it is difficult and I am at times unsuccessful, I think of my ex-husband as Lara's father *first* and my ex-husband

---

* Many excellent books deal with divorce. Several are listed in Appendix C.

The Planning Process

I. Preparation

(each co-parent, including stepparents, should complete this)

A. Agree on Time Frames

When will you complete the preparation?

When will you hold the meeting(s)?

B. Describe Your Child

List your child's strengths and weaknesses.

Hints: 1. Definition of child's disability.

2. Remember to include positive aspects such as creativity, athletic ability, musical talent, sense of humor, etc.

3. Talk to your child's brothers and sisters.

C. Set Goals

Thinking in terms of a six-month to one-year horizon, list two to five goals in each of the following categories (add or remove categories, if appropriate):

1. Behavior
2. Relationships
3. Living Skills
4. Academic
5. School

Hint: The Learning Style Questionnaire and Developmental Achievement Chart in *Negotiating the Special Education Maze* are good for categories 1–4.

D. Prioritize

Rank the goals developed above in order of importance.

Hints: 1. Be realistic.

2. Ask your child for ideas and opinions.

E. Develop Strategies

How can you help your child to achieve his or her goals?

Hints: 1. Remember what has worked for your child in the past.

2. Get input from your child.

continued...

F. Describe Your Child in Five Years

Think through your hopes and nightmares.

Hints: 1. Be realistic.

2. See the sample on page 11.

G. Describe Your Child at Age 22

Think through your hopes and nightmares.

Hints: 1. Be realistic.

2. See the sample on page 11.

H. Share with Your Co-Parent(s)

Discuss your plan with your co-parent.

II. Meeting

A. Strengths and Weakness

Create a consolidated list of your child's strengths and weaknesses.

B. Short-Term Goals

Select two to three goals and agree on how to achieve them. You may want to involve your children in this phase.

C. Five-Year Goals

Consolidate and agree on goals your child might achieve in five years.

D. Age-22 Goals

Consolidate and agree on goals your child might achieve by age 22.

III. Follow-Up

A. Share with Professionals

Share your plans for your child with the professionals who work with him or her.

B. Review

Review your plans for your child on a periodic basis. Some parents find that every six months is a good frequency for the one-year plan and that once-a-year reviews are good for the five-year and age-22 plans. Agree upon a frequency that works for you and your child.

second. In many ways I am fortunate because Skip has remained active in our daughter's life. But we have worked at that—we have both worked at keeping him involved. As Skip says, "You have to do a better job at dealing with differences than when you were married."

In some ways it is easier to be divorced. You don't have to eat together after an argument. You can hang up on an ex-spouse more easily than a spouse. You can put distance between you in times of tension simply by going home or hanging up the phone.

When Lara's father and I first separated several years ago, I used to think I was "winning" if my daughter did not spend all the agreed-upon time with her father. Then I realized that working with, instead of against, my ex-husband would ease the burden on me and be much better for Lara.

Communication can be more difficult when a child spends time in two homes. If your child has difficulty using language, communication problems can be compounded. Frequent phone calls and notes may be necessary. Lara brings a calendar back and forth between her two homes.

It is important to maintain communication not only between co-parents but also with the professionals working with your child. Noncustodial parents may not understand their child's needs as well because they do not spend as much time with their child. Participating in doctor's appointments, conferences, and team meetings helps to keep these parents actively involved in their child's lives.

Meetings that include divorced parents can be strained. Decide before the meeting where you want to be seated relative to your former spouse and discuss this with the meeting coordinator to enlist his or her assistance in getting you the seat you want. Using the services of a professional advocate during team meetings can also improve the communication between divorced parents.

If you have joint legal custody, both you and your ex-spouse have the right—and more importantly, the responsibility—to care for your child and to make sure that your child receives the best services possible.

3 Organizations

Children are like sponges, soaking up new information and new experiences. Like children, parents of children with disabilities typically are willing to listen to anyone who may be able to help them. Organizations can play a key role in providing information and support.

Organizations operate on several levels, offering various types of assistance. There are national, regional, and local groups. Some are affiliated with or funded by the government; others are independent. They may offer workshops, conferences, advocacy services, respite care, and literature. The most valuable aspect of these organizations is the opportunity they present to meet and talk with other parents. As one mother put it, "I get most of my information from other parents." Discussing your concerns and fears with other parents who may have gone through similar experiences can be comforting. Attending meetings also gives you a chance to meet professionals who may be working with your child or other children with similar needs.

Getting Started

Becoming affiliated with organizations that can provide information about your child's disability is an important first step. Support organizations exist for most diagnoses. The workshops, conferences, and literature provided by such groups keep parents and professionals up-to-date on home management and education strategies, as well as recent research findings. Because my daughter is learning disabled and has attention deficit disorder (ADD), I belong to the Learning Disabilities Association of America (LDA) and to Children and Adults with Attention Deficit Disorder (CH.A.D.D.), both of which give me insight into why Lara is who she is, and, more importantly, how I can help her reach her maximum potential.

Knowing your own and your child's rights under the law is as important as being knowledgeable about your child's disability. Parent Training and Information Centers (PTICs), funded by the federal government under Public Law 98-199 (the 1983 amendment to the Individuals with Disabilities Education Act, or IDEA), are found in each state (though they may have a name other than PTIC). PTICs provide training and literature on a state's special education laws and are required by law to conduct workshops and conferences that promote good working relationships between parents and professionals. Several state PTICs augment their federal funds with private contributions and memberships, and offer other services, such as advocacy, either for individual cases or for the disabled population in general. Your local and state special education offices can supply you with information regarding your state's PTIC.

Local parent groups can be an invaluable source of support. Many sponsor training workshops on state special education laws and related topics offered by PTICs, as well as on other topics of interest such as behavior management, promoting positive self-esteem, and inclusion strategies. State grants are often available to such organizations to help them provide teacher, parent, student, and community education programs. Hospitals also often provide community training, particularly on ADD and related problems.

Finding the Right Organization

The best place to begin your search for organizations that can provide support for you and your child is with the National

Information Center for Children and Youth with Disabilities (NICHY). NICHY is an information clearinghouse funded by the U.S. government. It provides listings of national organizations and listings of support organizations for each state.* Although most organizations ask that you pay a membership fee if you wish to receive newsletters and related information, they often host workshops and conferences that are open to the general public, usually at nominal cost. NICHY also responds to personal questions, makes referrals to other organizations, gives technical assistance to families and groups, and makes available countless publications of interest to parents, professionals, and individuals with disabilities. The publications cover topics ranging from specific disabilities to regulations and available services. All NICHY publications are available at no cost.

When Lara was first identified as having special needs, I sent letters to every organization for which I could get an address. Those organizations that could not be of service often referred me to others that could. When you send a query letter, provide as much information about your child as possible. Providing the diagnosis (or suspected diagnosis), your child's sex, age, and a description of the services your child is currently receiving can help the organization pinpoint the information most useful for you. (A sample letter appears on the next page.) Do not shy away from organizations because you think they cannot help you. For years I avoided contacting the Association for Retarded Citizens (ARC) because Lara is not mentally retarded. I missed a good source of support because ARC not only provides information regarding state regulations that apply to all children with disabilities, but also information on other resources.

Your local special education administrator should be able to give you contact names for local support groups. Some states, such as Massachusetts, mandate that each local school district have a Parent Advisory Council. In states where such groups are not established by law, many local support organizations have been formed through grass-roots initiatives.

---

* To help get you started on your search for the right organizations for you and your family, Appendix B provides a list of national organizations.

Sample Letter to an Organization

February 8, 1995

To Whom It May Concern:

I am the mother of a daughter who has a language disorder, is learning disabled, has ADD, and is of low-average intelligence. My daughter and I have inverted number 10 chromosomes. I am currently the cochair of a local Special Education Parent Advisory Council. At the present time I am working on a book for parents of children with disabilities on how to get the most out of their support network. I would appreciate any information your organization has that would be of potential benefit to me in any of my three roles! Thank you and I look forward to the receipt of the information.

Sincerely,

Lizanne Capper
123 Main Street
Anycity, USA 00000
555/555–5555

What Organizations Can Do for You

You may be feeling isolated, particularly if your child's disability has only recently been diagnosed. You may be hearing repeatedly from professionals that your child is unique. I heard this many times from a teacher of Lara's and thought, "Oh no, no one can help us!" Of course this was not the case. Each person is unique, whether disabled or not, but we also share common characteristics. The more I learned about learning disabilities and ADD, the more clearly I saw Lara emerge from the pages. I had to piece different words, sentences, ideas, theories, and descriptions together, but I finally "found" Lara.

You will not find another person whose situation is identical with yours, but you can find people who have or are facing similar obstacles. Those parents and children who have overcome adversity can be an inspiration, as well as a source of practical advice and information about available resources.

Hearing the experiences of other parents can also put things in perspective. As I listened to Julia,♦ the mother of four children, one learning disabled, one with ADD whose twin is autistic, I marveled at her energy and enthusiasm for life. My problems seemed small compared to hers. Another mother, Ellen, describes her experience at local meetings for parents of children with disabilities, where she learned that it's "O.K. not to be perfect":

I don't know what I would have done without them. I don't know that I would have been able to laugh or see the humor, or not be totally worried all the time.

In my early experience, I tended to be relatively quiet at parent meetings, absorbing as much as I could. As I have become more knowledgeable and self-assured over time, I offer advice and suggestions to other parents new to the world of children with disabilities. And I have seen my friend Ellen, who joined our local parent group a year after I did, grow through the same experience. So the cycle continues—parents helping parents to help their children.

Advocacy Services

PTICs, ARC, DREDF (Disability Rights Education and Defense Fund, Inc.), and countless other organizations offer advocacy services to children and adults with disabilities and their parents. Advocacy takes three primary forms: case, systems, and legislative. The most common is *case advocacy*, where a family member or professional advocate speaks out on behalf of a particular individual with disabilities. *Systems advocacy* refers to organized efforts to "change practices, rules, or regulations within a system, such as the local public schools or the city parks administration." Legislative advocacy refers to organized efforts to change "practices, rules, regulations, policies, and guidelines by making changes in laws."* Systems advocacy is often carried out by state and local organizations, whereas legislative advocacy is typically undertaken by state and national organizations. The Learning Disabilities Association of America (LDA), for example, was active in the drafting of, and lobbying for, the original federal special education law. LDA, along with many other national organizations, continues to participate actively in lobbying actions.

Each state also has a developmental disabilities planning council that functions as an advocacy organization for the developmentally disabled. A list of these councils is available from NICHY.

Professional case advocates operate on two levels. A professional advocate is intimately familiar with state regulations and knows the special education and transition-planning process and available resources. A professional advocate is also an impartial professional who can work with parents and the appropriate agencies to get the best possible services for a child with a disability. The best advocates will work themselves out of a job. While working with the parents, an advocate should be educating them to the point where the parents can advocate on their own. Advocates should impart knowledge about rights, laws, resources, programs, and negotiation techniques. Parents and people with disabilities should be able to champion their own cause after working with a professional advocate.

WHEN ARE ADVOCACY SERVICES NECESSARY?

Some advocates believe that every child should have an advocate. I agree: the parent should be the advocate. There are times, however, when the services of a professional advocate

---

* These definitions are from the Epilepsy Foundation of America series *Speaking Out, Partners in Advocacy: Understanding the Process*, (Landover, MD: Epilepsy Foundation of America, 1992), 18. *Speaking Out: Partners in Advocacy* is a comprehensive source of information on advocacy services. The three books in the series include *Understanding the Process, Family Action Guide*, and *Tools and Resources*. Although published by the Epilepsy Foundation of America (EFA), these books apply to all people with disabilities.

can be critical to obtaining the appropriate services for a person with a disability.

Parents of recently diagnosed children may need an advocate to educate and guide them during a time that is often filled with emotion. Absorbing federal, state, and local regulations and services can be overwhelming when parents are in the process of accepting their child's disability. Working with an advocate through the referral and initial evaluation and placement can reassure parents that their child will receive the appropriate services.

During times of transition (e.g., from a placement outside the home school district to a classroom within the community school) and times of conflict, a professional advocate can be a resource for programs and services, as well as for strategies and techniques that have worked for others. If your child will require services once he or she leaves school, an advocate can educate you and the school system about appropriate programs and agencies that can help.

When negotiations between parents and a government agency are strained, an advocate can offer an objective, third-party perspective. If you disagree with the school system about your child's placement, it may be appropriate to get an advocate. This is not always necessary, however. Often, the need for an advocate will depend on the readiness and willingness of the school system to listen and change.

Two mothers of autistic children in different school districts wanted their children included in general education classrooms. They did not want their children to be in substantially separate placements any longer. One set of parents went through the process with a professional advocate and eventually had to hire a lawyer. Their son is now thriving, integrated into the mainstream 100%. The other mother was able to work with her local special education administrator and school psychologist, and her daughter was successfully included in the local middle school.

FINDING AN ADVOCATE

As noted earlier, several organizations provide advocacy services. In some instances, the services of a case advocate are available at no charge or on a sliding fee scale. In addition to referring parents to particular individuals, advocacy organizations are available to answer questions and provide information over the telephone or through the mail. Local parent groups can often provide advocacy support on minor and even moderate issues. In dealing with the school system, it is beneficial to work with an advocate who has particular knowledge of your local school district.

It is important to work with an advocate with whom you can communicate and from whom you can learn. Ask other parents who have used the advocate for references. At your first meeting, discuss the role you expect the advocate to play. For example, you may want him or her to attend a team meeting with the school district primarily as an observer. You may want his or her advice following the meeting, rather than during it, or you may feel so overwhelmed and apprehensive that you want the advocate to participate actively in the meeting. Should you select this latter path, it is important to move away from this mode over time. A good advocate transfers knowledge and authority to the parent and possibly the person with disabilities.

Regardless of the role you want an advocate to play, it is critical that the advocate be a part of your child's team. All too often, advocates are viewed by public officials and others as adversaries, and indeed, some advocates have earned this label. Although a situation may be tense, approaching it as an adversary rather than as a team player is often counterproductive. If you do engage an advocate, make sure the team working with your child is aware of it and that the advocate is presented as a member of the team. If you plan to bring an advocate to a meeting, inform the other participants ahead of time. Reassure the team members that you have hired an advocate to make sure that your child gets the appropriate services and that you want to learn from the advocate. Put the services of the advocate in as positive a light as possible.

Respite Care

Respite care is professionally provided short-term care for people with disabilities. It is available for developmentally disabled people of any age, often at no or low cost, through various agencies. ARC provides respite care for developmentally disabled individuals in their own home, the care provider's home, or in a respite facility. Several states and communities have agencies that fund and provide trained respite caregivers.

Respite care can be used in times of emergency or for planned events. Some parents use respite care services regularly so that they can have time for themselves and can feel more comfortable knowing that their child is being cared for by a qualified individual. Some of these agencies now offer a "menu" of respite services, allowing families with children with disabilities more flexibility and choice.

Three national organizations provide information and guidance concerning respite care: Texas Respite Resource Network (TRRN), Access to Respite Care and Help (ARCH), and the National Respite Coalition. (Contact information is contained in Appendix B.) *Time Out for Families: Epilepsy and Respite Care*, published by the Epilepsy Foundation of America, is another excellent source of information about respite care. ARCH maintains a *National Respite Locator Service* for use by family members, professionals, and other interested individuals. Call 1–800/7–RELIEF (800/773–5433).

Ongoing Knowledge

Support organizations respond to the parents of children with disabilities because the organizations are run by parents and people with disabilities. I have been attending meetings, workshops, and conferences for over nine years, and although I sometimes ask myself, "Do I really need to go tonight? I'm tired and it's raining," I know that if I learn one thing from a two-hour workshop, a one-page article, or a 300-page book, it was worth my time. Or perhaps I don't learn something new but am reminded of something I should be doing or am reassured that what I am doing is right. If I can share my experience with another parent or with a professional, it is doubly worth it. Being involved in a support organization can help to channel your emotions to productive ends. I have become a better mother, better member of my community, and better member of my daughter's team by working to bring programs to my town that educate teachers, children, and parents about disabilities and about accepting and appreciating differences.

4 Working with Health Care Professionals

Depending on the nature of your child's disability, you may have regular to extensive interaction with various health care professionals. Your child may require extended care from physicians, therapists,* or mental health professionals. These services may be provided independently, through your school district, or through a state agency such as your state's department of mental health. The first section of this chapter will help you to select and work with health care professionals in general; it is followed by sections on working with pediatricians, other specialists, and mental health care professionals. Particularly in the area of mental health care provided by state agencies, parents often must negotiate aggressively for appropriate care.

Communication with health care professionals can be encumbered by many things, including language and emotions. People working in the health care field, particularly specialists, often seem to have a language all their own. The most effective way to surmount a communication obstacle is to ask questions and to keep asking them until they are answered in terms you understand. You may find, as I have, that it is helpful to bring an ongoing list of questions regarding your child to all appoint-

---

* Therapists in this context refers to professionals such as speech and language pathologists, occupational therapists, physical therapists, and so on.

ments. Reviewing the list of questions before the end of a meeting helps ensure that you do not walk out of an appointment with unanswered questions.

You may find it necessary to make an appointment for a longer consultation in order to get all of your questions answered. An alternative to this is following up your child's appointments with a phone call. It also helps to become knowledgeable in the area from a layman's perspective. You might ask a related support organization or the health care professional for recommendations on readings or other sources of information.

An important part of preparing for appointments with health care professionals is discussing them with your child. Be sure your child understands as best as possible when and why he or she is going to an appointment. Several children's books dealing with doctor's and hospital visits are available.

It is vital that you keep copies of all medical records, especially when your child sees several different health care professionals. Having the information readily available can facilitate the flow of information between health care providers and to new professionals. It also gives you a history of your child's treatment. Some parents find it beneficial to maintain a notebook with a record of, and notes from, all doctors' visits.

Finally, being open and honest with the people who provide care to your child is crucial to successful treatment. It is important to listen to their comments and suggestions. It is equally important to share with them your own observations and opinions. You are a critical member of your child's team and the health care professionals caring for your child must value your input and insight.

Building a Team to Care for Your Child

Children with some severe disabilities are predisposed to health problems as well as to other disabilities. Children with Down syndrome, for example, often have vision, dental, and heart problems, and other health difficulties. Children with cerebral palsy usually have at least one other disability such as a communication disorder, hearing loss, vision problem, seizure disorder, or mental retardation. People with learning disabilities are more likely than people in general to have ADD. Even if your child has only one disability, it is likely he or she will receive care from more than one health care professional.

The very nature of your child's disability may necessitate a multidisciplinary approach that includes using the services not only of health care specialists but education specialists as well. This is often true in the case of autism, where a child may be treated by a pediatrician for general health care, a pediatric dentist for normal dental care, a neurologist for a seizure disorder, a speech and language pathologist for speech and language therapy, a behavior specialist, and general and special educators. Some universities have multidisciplinary autism clinics, although in most cases these services are provided by several different sources. Every state has a medical treatment program called "Children with Special Health Needs" funded by the Maternal and Child Health Block Grant. (Contact information is provided in Appendix B.)

In some circumstances, your child's health care providers will work together on treatment; in others, they may not interact at all. Under either circumstance, it is critical for you to be the center of the team and to be a "case manager." Your child's pediatrician should also be a central player in many instances. Many parents are most comfortable when the pediatrician knows the specialists providing care for their child. This is of particular importance if your child is taking medication prescribed by different physicians. Your child's pediatrician should be consulted before your child begins taking new medications to avoid adverse drug reactions.

Because of the increased risk of hearing and visual impairments in children with disabilities, it is important that you have your child's hearing and vision tested early. Your child's pediatrician should recommend an audiologist or eye doctor (either an ophthalmologist or optometrist) for appropriate testing.

You and your child's health care providers must work as a team. As a parent, you are responsible for coordinating your child's care. With complex cases, including those where government agencies are involved, a case manager, usually on the staff of a state agency such as the department of mental health, may work closely with you to coordinate health care services. This coordination may include determining the appropriate setting for care, as well as negotiating who has financial responsibility for the care.

Pediatricians

Services to Expect

Your child's pediatrician is often the health care professional with whom your family has the longest relationship. He or she should be the core member of your child's health care team.* You should be aware, however, that pediatricians are usually not qualified to diagnose any disorders other than medical conditions. When the doctor suspects ADD, for example, no diagnosis is valid unless complete testing has been done (even if the pediatrician is also a psychiatrist). Although the pediatrician may not be able to diagnose a nonmedical disability, he or she is often among the first to suspect disabilities in a child and should help you determine when it is appropriate to contact the appropriate office in your state for early intervention services (see Chapter 5 for information regarding early intervention services).

If your child has medical needs that must be considered in educational or employment plans, your pediatrician should be willing to attend team meetings to see to it that these concerns are adequately handled.

Many parents of children with disabilities are frustrated by their pediatrician's lack of knowledge of special education and related services. In some instances, however, pediatricians are well informed about rights and services and pass this information to parents. My daughter's pediatrician began talking to

---

* Possible exceptions to this may be if your child's primary disability is an emotional, behavioral, or mental disorder.

me about early intervention services, which were available at that time in my state for children at age three, when Lara was 18 months old. We owe Lara's early start in special education in large part to the dedication of her pediatrician.

Finding the Right Pediatrician

Finding the right pediatrician for your family can be simple for some parents and quite difficult for others. The right pediatrician for your oldest child may not be right for your second or third child. Changes in the health of your children, or a move to a new community, may prompt or require you to find a new pediatrician.

Some parents decide to change pediatricians after their child is diagnosed as having a disability. You and your child's pediatrician may have disagreed over the possible presence of a disability prior to a formal diagnosis being made and your confidence in the physician may have eroded, causing you to look elsewhere for care. Your child may have a disability with which the pediatrician has little or no experience. If your child is also seen by competent specialists, your pediatrician's lack of experience may not be cause for a change, but many parents are most comfortable working with a pediatrician who has a good knowledge of their child's disability.

Although the American Academy of Pediatrics and your insurance company can provide assistance in selecting a pediatrician, other parents are often the best source of information. Talking with parents gives you the opportunity to get questions answered from a perspective close to your own. If your child has special medical needs, it is especially helpful for you to talk with other parents in similar circumstances. You should also interview the prospective pediatricians before making your decision. Suzanne Ripley's *A Parents' Guide to Doctors, Disabilities, and the Family* (published by NICHY) contains a good set of questions to ask of the doctors you are considering for your child's care.

If you do not feel comfortable with your child's current pediatrician, consider making a change. Be sure to be honest with yourself about wanting to find a new doctor, however. When your pediatrician is telling you something that you do not want to hear, ask yourself if a change is in the best interest of your child.

Maintaining a Good Relationship and Getting Quality Care

In some circumstances, your child's pediatrician may be one of your strongest sources of support. Maintaining a good relationship with him or her can raise the quality of that support. Being well-prepared for appointments and asking questions either during appointments or as a follow-up can help you develop and maintain such a relationship. As is true in your relationship with other professionals, it is important to remember that you are an expert on your own child. If you are concerned about your child's development or health, push for answers and trust your instincts. Do not accept statements such as "she'll grow out of it." Early intervention increases a child's opportunity for success. According to Dr. Mark Batshaw, in *Your Child Has A Disability*, valuable time is lost for many mildly mentally retarded children, most of whom are not diagnosed until kindergarten or first grade. Occupational and physical therapies, for example, are most effective if started early, when the central nervous system is still developing.

When a child has intensive medical needs, it is easy to miss developmental issues.

Ellen, whose daughter Elizabeth, has Turner's syndrome and underwent many operations at a young age, in part blames Elizabeth's pediatrician for missing her developmental delays. The doctor and parents were so focused on Elizabeth's medical problems that she did not start receiving early intervention services until she was four years old, one year later than she was eligible for them.

Marcy continually pointed out to Jacob's pediatrician that her son was missing developmental milestones. Jacob, now seven, may be mildly mentally retarded and has a seizure disorder, ADD, and dyspraxia, and is hypotonic.

Specialists

There are many types of medical and professional specialists, including, among others, audiologists, behavior therapists, neuropsychologists, neurologists, child development specialists, nutritionists, respiratory therapists, orthopedic surgeons, physiatrists, geneticists, genetic counselors, and augmentative communication specialists. Depending upon the needs of your child, you may encounter none or many of these professionals. Regardless of the professional's expertise, anyone working with your child should be a *pediatric* specialist as well as experienced with your child's particular disability or combination of disabilities. Some pediatric dentists, for example, are trained in caring for children with disabilities.

Your child's pediatrician is most likely to be the one who refers you to a particular specialist. Parents of children with similar problems, however, are also good sources of information about specialists, as are support groups and professional case advocates. Under all circumstances, you should keep in mind the limits of your health insurance policy and the ramifications your choices may have on coverage.

In addition to the above sources, information is available to you on particular types of specialists from several organizations. For example, the American Speech and Hearing Association (ASHA) publishes listings of audiologists and speech and language pathologists with experience in pediatrics. The U.S. Department of Health and Human Services in Washington, D.C., publishes a booklet, *Comprehensive Clinical Genetic Services Centers*, that can help you locate genetic counseling services. The staff members of these centers typically include a genetic counselor, a geneticist, and an obstetrician.

ADD clinics are becoming increasingly available at hospitals. These clinics often provide such services as pediatric neurology, behavior management training, social skills training, parent support groups, school consultation, parent and community education, medication monitoring, and family and individual counseling.

Most hospitals also offer audiology services. In addition to performing and evaluating hearing tests, audiologists can help parents locate appropriate programs for their children. It is recommended that hearing be tested by the age of six to seven months in children who are developmentally disabled or delayed, premature, have a chromosomal abnormality, have recurrent ear infections, or whose mothers had intrauterine infections. If your child suffers from a mild hearing loss, even if it is expected to be temporary, he or she should have frequent speech and language evaluations. These are often performed at hospitals, but are also available from independent speech and language pathologists. For children between the ages of six months and three years, evaluations should be conducted every three months; children three years and older should be evaluated every six months.*

Children with disabilities are also at increased risk for vision impairments. Eyesight should be tested as early as six months of age and frequently thereafter so that any necessary corrections can be made. If your child has a language disorder, it is important for the doctor checking his or her vision to understand the ramifications of this or any other disability. If you believe your son or daughter's disabilities are not being adequately considered, discuss this with the doctor. If this does not work out satisfactorily, find another physician.

> *Although I was certain my daughter needed vision correction, our first eye doctor repeatedly advised me to wait. After visits every four months for a year, I decided to get a second opinion. Lara now wears pink glasses to correct a crossed eye and severe farsightedness.*

If your child has physical disabilities or severe communication disorders, technology can play a critical role in giving him or her independence. Adaptive equipment facilitates mobility and communication. Depending on the nature of the disability, a number of specialists may participate in recommending, selecting, and fitting this equipment, and training you and your child

---

* Batshaw, M. L., *Your Child Has A Disability* (Little, Brown and Company, 1991).

in its use. An occupational therapist, physical therapist, speech and language pathologist, or other professional may work with your child and you in this area. All specialists should be able to help parents locate potential funding sources for the equipment and appropriate fitting and training. Much of the equipment available today can be customized—your child may even be able to select "designer" colors!

> *A simple pink basket attached to the front of Catherine's◆ walker made it easier for the four-year-old (who has a muscle disorder) to accept and use her new equipment.*

Effective Communication

Communication is a two-way street, but there are steps you can take to improve the likelihood of effective communication among you, your child, and your child's specialists. In addition to reviewing the suggestions made at the beginning of this chapter, consider some of the tips presented below, which are unique to working with specialists. Communication is a factor in preparing for, attending, and following up on the appointments.

PREPARING FOR AN APPOINTMENT

If your child sees more than two or three specialists, it is particularly helpful to keep a schedule of appointments. I maintain a chart listing the type of physician, name, phone number, date of last visit, frequency of visits, and date of the next appointment. (A sample chart appears on the next page). Not only does it help me keep track of Lara's appointments, it also facilitates communication with my ex-husband.

Before an appointment with a specialist, particularly if the appointment is a first visit, you should prepare a list of questions and review it with your child's pediatrician, an advocate, friend, family member, or co-parent. In the case of older children, you may also want to discuss with your child his or her questions, as well as your own.

If your child will be seen by a health care professional in a field in which you are unfamiliar, reading up on the discipline before the first appointment can be useful. Ask your child's

Lara's Physician Schedule

Doctor/Type	Frequency	Last Visit	Next Visit
Moyns♦ (pediatrician)	annually	10/19/94	11/11/95
Koins♦ (dentist)	6 months	9/11/94	3/95
Michaels♦ (neurologist)	6 months	3/15/95	11/11/95
Owen♦ (eye)	as needed	9/14/94	1/11/95
Audiology Dept. (audiologist)	annually	9/8/94	11/11/95
Fitzgerald♦ (genetic counselor)	as needed		
Neurodevelopmental Center (psychological evaluation)	3 years	3/1/92	3/95

pediatrician to recommend reading material. Your local library may also be helpful.

ATTENDING THE APPOINTMENT

I recall with anxiety our visit to a geneticist (Lara and I have inverted number ten chromosomes, but the specialists see no connection to Lara's disabilities). I was unprepared to see a sign reading "Birth Defects" identifying the department. I relied too heavily on my ex-husband (who has a degree in chemistry and understood the lingo better than I) to interpret what the geneticist was saying. Looking back on that appointment, I wished I had been more assertive in getting my own questions answered and had asked my daughter's pediatrician what the meeting would be like.

Medical specialists tend to be technical in their outlook and may have weaker interpersonal skills than pediatricians. It is easy to be intimidated by their knowledge and jargon. Remember, however, that they are providing a service to *you*, and you and your child are the customers. Do not be afraid to ask questions or to ask the specialist to repeat or rephrase things in lay terms.

Many parents find it helpful to attend appointments with medical specialists together, especially the initial appointment. If your co-parent is unable or unwilling to attend, bring a family member or friend. Not only is it advantageous to have another person to absorb the information, ask questions, and take notes, but you may need each other's emotional support. If your co-parent cannot attend, consider taping the session so that your co-parent may hear the information accurately.

When a doctor suspects that a child may have mental retardation, cerebral palsy, or autism, he or she may hesitate to tell the parents, either because of uncertainty over the diagnosis and or because of a desire not to unnecessarily upset or hurt the parents.

One neurologist lamented to a mother after he finally formally diagnosed her son as autistic: "I just couldn't bring myself to tell you. I just couldn't. I'm sorry."

Parents in most cases want to know the truth. They want as much information as possible. The unknown may result in unfounded fears and inappropriate expectations, or worse, can result in inappropriate decisions being made.

A director of special education recalled with sadness the day she realized that the parents of a ten-year-old girl in her class had never been told their daughter was mentally retarded.

The term *developmental delay* is frequently used for children who are suspected of being mentally retarded or autistic, or of having cerebral palsy. In the case of suspected cerebral palsy, developmental delay is often used in children from birth to six months of age. Developmental delay is frequently used until ages two through five when autism or mental retardation is suspected. According to Dr. Mark Batshaw in *Your Child Has a Disability*, the label "developmentally delayed" is inappropriate for children over the age of two or three. If this term is used to describe your child, ask the question, "Do you think my child has cerebral palsy, is mentally retarded, or is autistic?" If the physician is not yet ready to make a formal diagnosis, find out how and when he or she plans to do so. Once your child has reached the age of three or four and is still labeled developmentally delayed, you may want to consider getting a second opinion. Do not be afraid to ask.

> *My daughter was labeled "developmentally delayed" at approximately ten months of age. It was not until Lara had a comprehensive psychological evaluation at a local hospital when she was seven years old that I had the courage to ask if that term meant she was mentally retarded. Even though I was certain it did not in Lara's case, I needed to hear it from a professional to relieve some of my anguish. Specialists will often assume that you know what a particular IQ score means. It was not until I met with the psychologist who conducted the evaluation that I asked and found out that an IQ of 80 is considered on the low end of average (Lara had received that same score during a test done two years earlier).*

Medical terms often change over time. As the result of continued research and new discoveries, changes are made so that conditions and disabilities are better described. Mongolism became Down syndrome many years ago; minimal brain dysfunction eventually became learning disability; pervasive developmental delay now describes a certain type of autism; and seizure disorder is replacing epilepsy. If a doctor uses an unfamiliar diagnosis, ask him or her if the term used to describe your child now was once called something else. Unfortunately, doctors will not always offer this information unsolicited.

Marcy and Ben, whose son has a seizure disorder, did not realize this was a new term for epilepsy. Having this connection made for them in the beginning would have heightened their understanding of Jacob's disability.

FOLLOWING UP ON THE APPOINTMENT

When a person is seen by a medical specialist, a letter describing the findings of the appointment and any associated tests is typically sent to the primary care physician. These letters are often helpful to the patient as well, or in the case of a child, to the parents. Before leaving an appointment with a specialist, ask that a copy of this letter be mailed to you. Bring a self-addressed, stamped envelope if necessary. In some cases, a written evaluation will be produced. Upon reviewing this or any other related documentation, be certain to get discrepancies or misunderstandings clarified.

If your child is placed on medication, it is important to inform his or her school, if applicable, and to work closely with the prescribing physician to monitor the effects of the medication. With some medication, such as Ritalin, it is critical to get feedback from your child's teacher. The doctor who prescribed the medication should be able to recommend effective means of obtaining information from your child's teachers or other appropriate people.

With certain diagnoses, further testing may be called for. For example, if mental retardation is the diagnosis, chromosome testing should be performed. This may result in identification of the cause of the mental retardation or other health problems. If your child is diagnosed with ADD, it is important to determine if there are coexisting disabilities such as learning disabilities, emotional disturbances, or obsessive/compulsive disorder.

When To Stop Asking Why and Begin Focusing on Treatment

In some cases, it is important to look for the cause of a child's disability. A chromosomal basis for your child's disability, for example, could influence your decisions regarding future pregnancies. A specific cause can help some parents better accept their child's disability. With many children with disabilities, however, the underlying cause remains a mystery. The cause of spina bifida, 50% of hearing losses, most learning disabilities, ADD, and many cases of mental retardation are unknown.

A complete diagnosis should include the determination of cause and an opinion or conclusion as to what the disability is. It is important to recognize that no matter what the cause of your child's disability, it is the *manifestation* of that disability and the combination of your child's abilities that should drive treatment, both medical and educational. Children with Down syndrome, a disability for which the cause is known, are educated quite differently depending on their level of intelligence, communication skills, and other factors. All children and parents have a right to a diagnosis and prognosis, however.

Jane♦ was relieved when the formal diagnosis of autism was made for her son after seven years of anguish and unanswered questions.

Mental Health Professionals

The decision to seek the services of a mental health professional is a personal one. Some people are very comfortable with the idea of psychotherapy, others would never consider this an option. Your child's teacher, pediatrician, or someone else who works with your child may suggest counseling. Ultimately, however, the decision is yours and it is important that you and your child feel ready.

Therapy can give you and your family an opportunity to reflect. You may find that you have trouble coping with the stress of being the parent of a child with disability and you may benefit from individual or couple therapy. Children can benefit from therapy if they have a poor self-image or low self-esteem. Unfortunately, these emotional considerations are not uncommon to children with disabilities, especially invisible ones such as learning disabilities or ADD.

Behavior problems are common in children with disabilities. Therapists can work with children and parents to develop appropriate behavior management programs. There are therapists who specialize in this area and many hospitals have behavior management clinics.

Independent Evaluations

A psychologist can perform a psychological evaluation of your child. Some parents take this route when they disagree with a school psychologist's assessment. Other parents want their child evaluated only once and have more confidence in an independent evaluator than in the school personnel. They have an outside professional conduct the testing in place of the school psychologist. If you opt for this approach, be aware that you will most likely be responsible for the cost of the outside evaluation. Insurance options should be discussed with your child's pediatrician.

Whatever your motivation for an independent evaluation, discuss your objectives with the evaluator. Those objectives might be: a recommendation regarding your child's educational placement, justification for socialization goals and objectives on your child's IEP (Individualized Education Plan), or perhaps a lack of trust in the results of an IQ test and the desire for a second opinion.

If you plan to use the written report produced by the evaluator when negotiating for services for your child, it is important to work with the evaluator on the documentation. Before testing begins, the evaluator should understand how you plan to use the report and be willing to work with you to refine it. Independent evaluators will often attend team meetings. If you want this to happen, secure the agreement of the team before the assessment begins.

Selecting a Counselor/Therapist

Several different types of professionals provide counseling services, including psychologists, psychiatrists, social workers, clergy, and specialists such as art therapists. The most important requirement is that the counselor and your child be able to communicate. There must be trust between you and the counselor as well. In addition to these requirements (which are necessary whether the client has a disability or not) the counselor must have an understanding of your child's disability and have strategies for compensating for it in counseling sessions. If your child has a communication disorder, it is important that the therapist have had previous experience in this area. Have a prospective therapist explain how he or she would work with your child, and share ideas and techniques that have worked for you or for others dealing with your child.

As you may have done when selecting other professionals, it is a good idea for you to talk with other parents about therapists they have used. Their opinions and experiences may steer you away from disaster and toward success. Also bear in mind that sometimes there will not be a good fit even with a good counselor and you may have to shop around. We tried four therapists before finding the right one for us.

Getting Started

Before embarking on therapy or counseling, decide what your expectations are. Talking these over with your co-parent, child, and prospective therapist/counselor can get you off to a good start. Children who are apprehensive about attending therapy sessions should be reassured that going for counseling or therapy does not mean that they are "crazy." Be specific with your child about why you think therapy will be of benefit. For example, if your objective is to improve your child's behavior, tell your child so. Give him or her an example of a specific behavior you would like to change and why. Explain what the first session will be like and that it is being undertaken to help him or her.

Working with Your Child's Therapist

The key to working with any mental health professional is honesty. Share information about your child, yourself, and your family with the therapist. The counselor should have copies of IEPs, IFSPs (Individual Family Service Plans), your plans for your child, and evaluation results. If your child is on medication, ask the therapist if having your child take it prior to the appointment might make the difference between an ineffective meeting and a productive meeting. Similarly, try to schedule your child's appointments for those times of the day when you know he or she will be most relaxed, focused, and responsive.

Follow up with your child's therapist after appointments. Some parents find it helpful to schedule a separate session without their child to discuss their child's progress. The therapist should be a willing and active participant on your child's team, attending meetings or providing periodic written reports. If your child is older, be certain to appreciate your child's right to privacy, however. Your child may not want you or anyone else discussing the therapy. As long as your child appears to benefit from counseling, an assertion of privacy from your child should be taken as a positive step toward independence.

5 Rights and Services under Federal Law

When I was young I received special education services. I had a terrible time pronouncing "s" and "z," and in second grade attended speech therapy in my school's basement. From third grade on, my teachers helped me overcome dyslexia. I was fortunate—my school system took care of my needs and I did well in school. Most children with disabilities in my generation were not nearly so lucky. The law has played a dramatic role in making sure that special education and related services are available to children with disabilities. It also protects the rights of and provides services to adults with disabilities.

Over 60 federal laws affect individuals with disabilities. In turn, each state has legislation and regulations that carry out these federal mandates. In all cases state law must comply with federal law; in some cases, though, states go above and beyond the requirements of federal legislation. Each local school system also has regulations and procedures of its own that must comply with—but can go beyond—state law.

Knowing Your Rights

To be certain that your child receives the best services possible, you must know your rights. This knowledge will give you the power and confidence to be a stronger advocate for your child. In some cases, you may need to be familiar with only one law, but if your child has multiple or severe disabilities, you will need to know about several pieces of legislation. Most laws affecting people with disabilities, such as the Americans with Disabilities Act, protect individual rights. Other laws, such as the Individuals with Disabilities Education Act (IDEA), provide protection of rights as well as funding for services. These laws are well intended, but *you* must make them work for your child.

Sources of Learning

This chapter provides an overview of the major laws affecting people with disabilities. There are many sources of additional information. Although the laws themselves are available to the general public, they are a bit overwhelming to digest. Several organizations provide overviews and summaries of the various pieces of legislation; most of these organizations also offer training for parents in the form of workshops. There are also other books that provide in-depth coverage of specific laws affecting individuals with disabilities (see Appendix C).

The Office of Special Education and Rehabilitative Services of the U.S. Department of Education's *Summary of Existing Legislation Affecting People with Disabilities* provides an overview of the federal statutes affecting disabled individuals. The office also has available a *Pocket Guide to Federal Help for Individuals with Disabilities*. These publications may be obtained by writing to the Clearinghouse on Disability Information (see Appendix C).

No matter what your child's age or disability, you must be familiar with the laws in your state. Some states provide summaries of specific pieces of legislation (available by contacting your state representative). Your state department of special education is also a good source of information. Organizations such as the Association for Retarded Citizens (ARC) and state Parent Training and Information Centers (PTIC) also offer training on specific state laws. Chapter 3 has additional information on these organizations.

Several books provide an in-depth review of specific pieces of legislation. One such book, *Negotiating the Special Education Maze,* by Winifred Anderson, Stephen Chitwood, and Deidre Hayden, covers thoroughly the federal special education law. The book also contains excellent recommendations on working effectively with your school system.

Federal Legislation: A Summary

The two primary pieces of federal legislation that concern children and young adults with disabilities are the Individuals with Disabilities Education Act (IDEA) and the Rehabilitation Act of 1973. Public Law 99-457, now incorporated into IDEA, details the Early Intervention Services available for eligible children from birth through age five.

IDEA and the Rehabilitation Act: A Comparison

IDEA protects the rights of children ages three to 21 to special education and related services. The Rehabilitation Act of 1973 protects the rights of children with disabilities throughout their time in school and provides training, support, and counseling to eligible individuals throughout adulthood.

The two laws differ greatly as to eligibility. IDEA is an entitlement law. This means that children who meet the law's requirements have an absolute right to receive special education and related services. The Rehabilitation Act of 1973 allows states to develop their own policies on how and to whom to provide services. The Rehabilitation Act requires that priority be given to those persons with the most severe disabilities, and most states do so. Although there is no automatic entitlement to services, certain rights are given protection under the Rehabilitation Act.

Regardless of the law under which your child is receiving services, you must consider yourself a partner in the planning, decision-making, and execution of those services. Under IDEA, your right to do so is protected by law. To a certain extent, these rights are protected under the Rehabilitation Act as well. The extent to which you exercise your rights under the latter law will depend on your child's age and how well he or she can self-advocate. In all cases, you have the right to request that outside specialists working with your child be on your child's evaluation teams. Evaluation teams are critical to the initial eligibility decision. Once eligibility is determined, the evaluation team makes recommendations for the types of services to be provided for your child, and in some cases for your family. If your child has been seen by an independent professional and you feel that this individual can add value to the evaluation process (whether under IDEA or the Rehabilitation Act), you have a right to have that person included.

When planning your child's school experience, it is important to remember that IDEA, as well as Section 504 of the Rehabilitation Act, protect your child's right to participate in all nonacademic and extracurricular activities, including recess, sports, and clubs. Section 504 requires that a student's disability be taken into consideration in determining eligibility for school sports. For example, if a child is receiving special education services and his or her grades fall below the requirement for sports activities, special allowances must be made.

Other Federal Legislation

Although IDEA and the Rehabilitation Act are the most important federal laws for children and young adults with disabilities, it is helpful to understand other legislation that may affect your child. For example, there are specific laws that may provide your child with services if he or she is developmentally disabled or visually or hearing impaired. The list on pages 60 and 61 provides a snapshot of federal laws affecting people with disabilities and indicates the ages each law covers and the severity of needs each law addresses. Public Law 99–457, although now included within IDEA, is listed separately because it supports a particular group of children. Of the laws listed, this chapter presents detailed information on Early Intervention Services (Public Law 99–457, now Part H of IDEA), IDEA (Public Law 102–119), and the Rehabilitation Act of 1973, along with four other federal laws.

Early Intervention Services

Summary and Eligibility

In 1986, the Early Intervention Services mandate was brought about by the passage of Public Law 99-457, a funding and rights law now incorporated into Part H of IDEA. Public Law 99-457 requires the provision of services to children from birth through age five. Infants and toddlers (from birth through age two) are covered by a program for developmentally disabled and developmentally delayed children and their families. Preschool children (ages three through five) with disabilities are eligible for special education and related services. These same services are available to children ages six through 21 under IDEA.

States are at varying stages of implementing Early Intervention Services. Some states, such as New Mexico, have chosen not to receive federal aid and thus do not offer Early Intervention Services. These states currently provide services only to children from ages six through 21.

Important Points

Public Law 99-457 (incorporated into Part H of the Individuals with Disabilities Education Act in 1991) provides for special education and related services to children from birth through age five. It is unique in that it extends certain services to the family of the child. An Individual Family Service Plan (IFSP) is developed for each eligible child and his or her family. The IFSP defines the Early Intervention Services to be provided. The services can include education, respite care, health care, in-home family support, physical therapy, occupational therapy, and speech and language therapy.

Early Intervention Services are coordinated by a case manager. During the child's infancy, the case manager, home teacher, and appropriate therapists visit the child and parent(s) in the home, usually on a weekly basis. The team works together to develop a program unique to the child's needs as defined in the IFSP. Parents are provided with instruction so that they can supplement the program between team visits.

Federal Laws Affecting People with Disabilities

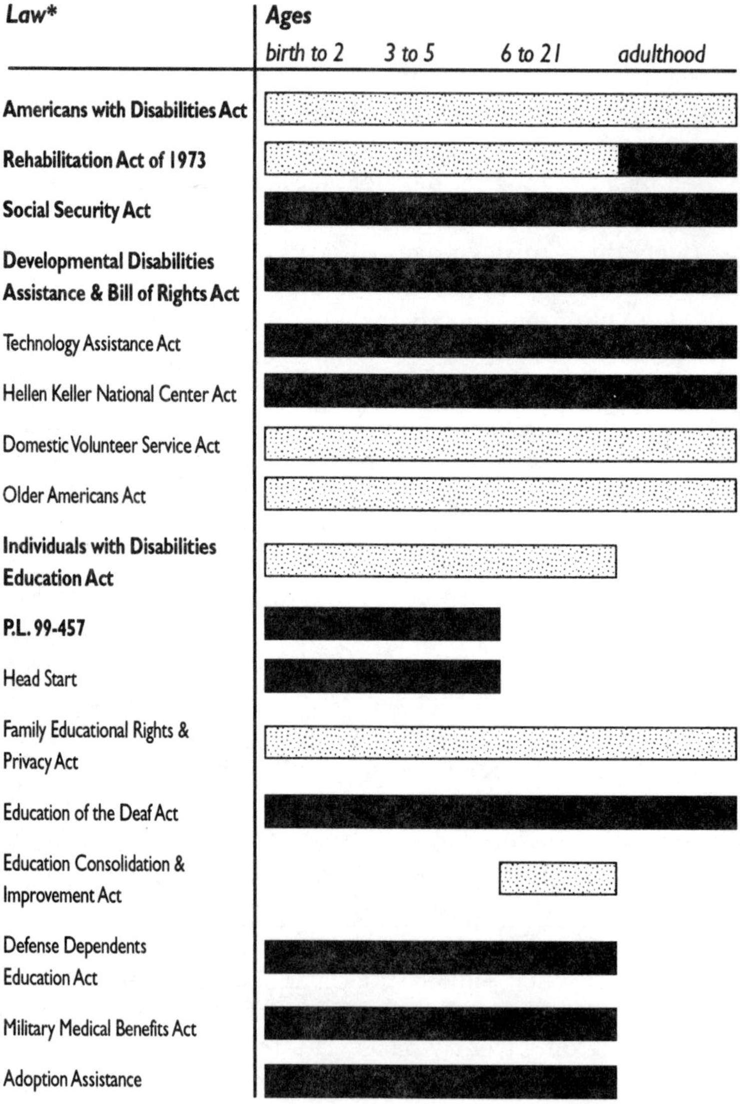
Law*
Ages
birth to 2
3 to 5
6 to 21
adulthood
Americans with Disabilities Act
Rehabilitation Act of 1973
Social Security Act
Developmental Disabilities Assistance & Bill of Rights Act
Technology Assistance Act
Hellen Keller National Center Act
Domestic Volunteer Service Act
Older Americans Act
Individuals with Disabilities Education Act
P.L. 99-457
Head Start
Family Educational Rights & Privacy Act
Education of the Deaf Act
Education Consolidation & Improvement Act
Defense Dependents Education Act
Military Medical Benefits Act
Adoption Assistance

continued...

Federal Laws Affecting People with Disabilities

Law*	Ages			
	birth to 2	*3 to 5*	*6 to 21*	*adulthood*
National Library Service Act			████████████████	
Architectural Barriers Removal Act			▓▓▓▓▓▓▓▓▓▓▓▓▓▓▓▓▓▓▓▓	
Urban Mass Transportation Act			▓▓▓▓▓▓▓▓▓▓▓▓▓▓▓▓▓▓▓▓	
Federal-Aid Highway Act			▓▓▓▓▓▓▓▓▓▓▓▓▓▓▓▓▓▓▓▓	
Rail Passenger Service Act			▓▓▓▓▓▓▓▓▓▓▓▓▓▓▓▓▓▓▓▓	
Federal Aviation Act			▓▓▓▓▓▓▓▓▓▓▓▓▓▓▓▓▓▓▓▓	
Javits-Wagner-O'Day Act				████████
Randolph-Sheppard Act				████████
Job Training Partnership Act				████████
Fair Labor Standards Act				████████
Small Business Act				████████
Wagner-Payser Act				████████
United States Housing Act of 1937				████████
Housing Act of 1949				████████
National Affordable Housing Act				████████
Fair Housing Act				████████

affects all persons with disabilities	░░░░░░░░░░░░░░░░
for persons with specific disabilities	████████████████
for persons with physical disabilities	▓▓▓▓▓▓▓▓▓▓▓▓▓▓▓▓

* Laws in boldface are covered in this chapter.

As the infant becomes a toddler, he or she may visit an Early Intervention Center two or three days a week for a structured program. Continued parent training is given as required so that parents remain active participants in the program. A case manager coordinates these services throughout the child's participation in Early Intervention Services.

Public Law 99–457 also mandates that children with hearing loss receive services beginning in infancy by speech and language pathologists or educators for the hearing impaired. The law also mandates the provision of services for testing hearing, fitting hearing aids, and follow-up care.

Because the services available to developmentally disabled and delayed infants and toddlers are so diverse, a great deal of collaboration among health, social service, and educational agencies is necessary. The governor of each state designates an agency to administer Early Intervention Services. This agency is responsible for coordinating the services of the other agencies, ensuring that the needs of the child are met. Each state must also operate a Child Find program to seek out children with disabilities from birth through age three. Child Find offices are also available to receive initial inquiries about special education. A listing of your state's Child Find office(s) is available from your state's office of special education.

In addition to complying with the federal laws, each state establishes its own laws governing the rights and services extended. Most states stay close to the federal mandates, but some offer additional services and rights. For example, each state has its own definition of developmental delay. If your child has been diagnosed as developmentally delayed, it is important to be familiar with your state's definition to determine if your child is eligible for Early Intervention Services. Your pediatrician or child's neurologist, as well as your state's Child Find office, can help with this. Your state may also extend services to children who are *at risk* for developmental delay. For example, premature infants are at risk for developmental delay and may qualify for Early Intervention Services in your state even before a medical diagnosis is made. Again, the Child Find office or your child's doctor can provide information to you.

Your state must also maintain a central directory of Early Intervention Services, from which you can learn about the types of services available, as well as where and how they are delivered in your state. The directory should be accessible at Child Find offices and the agency designated to run Early Intervention Services in your state. Under Public Law 99–457, your state is also required to run public awareness campaigns to inform pediatricians and others working with infants and toddlers about the availability of Early Intervention Services.

When a child who is receiving Early Intervention Services turns three, he or she usually begins attending a special education preschool. Most are within local community schools and are language-based classrooms. (The services provided to children ages three to five are covered under IDEA later in this chapter.)

Learning More About Early Intervention Services

The Child Find office in your state should be able to provide you with all the necessary information regarding Early Intervention Services. If you are unsure of how or if you should contact this office, discuss the idea with your pediatrician. He or she should be able to confirm whether or not your child might be eligible for Early Intervention Services (see Chapter 4 for a discussion on working with pediatricians). The special education department in your state or local community can also provide information regarding Early Intervention Services. The Association for Retarded Citizens (ARC) is also a good resource (see Chapter 3 for more information regarding ARC).

The Individuals with Disabilities Education Act

The Individuals with Disabilities Education Act (IDEA)* is the primary source of federal aid to state and local school systems for special education and related services. Its purpose is to:

assure that all children with disabilities have available to them, within the time periods specified…a free appropriate public education which emphasizes special edu-

---

* Formerly the Education for All Handicapped Children Act (P.L. 94-142).

cation and related services designed to meet their unique needs, to assure that the rights of children with disabilities and their parents or guardians are protected, to assist states and localities to provide for the education of all children with disabilities, and to assess and assure the effectiveness of efforts to educate children with disabilities.

IDEA is both a funding and a rights law. Some of the funding is formula-based, that is, each state is given a certain level of funding based on a common formula. Other funding is available through grants for which various organizations, including local and state agencies, can apply. IDEA also protects the rights of your child and your rights as a parent.

The Education for All Handicapped Children Act (Public Law 94-142) was the predecessor of IDEA. Prior to its passage in November 1975, special education services were offered at the discretion of state and local education authorities. The Act has been amended several times since its passage, but the most important amendment came in October 1990 with the enactment of IDEA. The major changes in the law include:

- The word *disabled* was substituted for the word *handicapped* throughout the law.

- The definition of *children with disabilities* was expanded to include autism and traumatic brain injury.

- The settings in which special education can be offered were clarified.

- *Transition services* for children leaving special education are now defined as: a coordinated set of activities for a student, designed within an outcome-oriented process, which promotes movement from school to post-school activities, including post-secondary education, vocational training, integrated employment (including supported employment), continuing and adult education, adult services, independent living or community participation. The coordinated set of activities shall be based upon the individual student's needs, and includes instruction, community experiences, the development of employment and other post-school adult living objectives, and when appropriate, acquisition of daily living skills and functional vocational evaluation.

- An individualized transition plan must be developed and incorporated into the IEP (Individualized Education Plan) when a student reaches age 16 (or younger if appropriate).

Eligibility

With the inclusion of Public Law 99–457 (the statute covering Early Intervention Services) in IDEA, children from birth through age 21 are now covered by federal law. Each state has its own laws covering special education and Early Intervention Services. States receiving funds under Part H of the act must provide services to children from birth through age two and their families. To qualify for federal funding under Section 619 of IDEA, states must provide services to children ages three through five. It is important that you become familiar with the specific laws of your state. Each state, for example, has its own eligibility guidelines for special education and related services. Most states make these guidelines available in layman's terms to the general public. Copies of your state laws and associated eligibility guidelines are available from your state department of education's office of special education.

Some states may also provide additional information. For example, the Massachusetts Department of Education, Division of Special Education, publishes the following documents in addition to the special education regulations: *A Parent's Guide to the Special Education Regulations, Parents' Rights Brochure, Eligibility Guidelines for Special Education*, and *A Parent's Guide to the Special Education Appeals Process.*

Legislation Regarding ADD

The inclusion of attention deficit disorder (ADD) as a disabling condition has caused controversy in many school systems. In September 1991, the U.S. Department of Education published an *ADD Policy Clarification Memorandum* that stated: "children with

ADD should be classified as eligible for services under the 'other health impaired' category in instances where the ADD is a chronic or acute health problem that results in limited alertness, which adversely affects educational performance." To qualify for services under the other category of health impairment, a child must exhibit 'limited strength, vitality, or alertness, due to chronic or acute health problems (such as ...) which adversely affects a child's educational performance."

This document reinforces Part B of IDEA and asserts that a child may not be denied an evaluation solely because the child's only diagnosis is ADD. It also maintains that simply having ADD does not qualify a student for special education services. ADD must be adversely affecting the child's performance in school in order for the child to qualify for special education services.

If your school system finds your child ineligible for special education under IDEA, his or her rights may still be protected by Section 504 of the Rehabilitation Act. Section 504 is civil rights legislation that prohibits discrimination against individuals with disabilities by organizations utilizing federal funds. You may be able to argue successfully that your child's civil rights are being violated if special education is not provided to accommodate for his or her ADD. Section 504 also protects your child's right to have classroom modifications made to accommodate for a disability. According to the U.S. Department of Education memorandum, classroom modifications can include "providing a structured learning environment, repeating and simplifying instructions about in-class and homework assignments, supplementing verbal instructions with visual ones, using behavior management techniques, adjusting class schedules, modifying test delivery, tailoring homework assignments, posting and reviewing rules regularly, giving preparation before transitions, finding ways to reduce writing assignments, increasing salience of critical information, and shortening length of bus rides."

Important Points

IDEA has six important components. Although each state may have its own regulations, all states must comply with the following rules:

1. FREE APPROPRIATE PUBLIC EDUCATION. The law states that all children will be provided with an appropriate public education, at no cost to their parents, regardless of disability. Children cannot be denied services because there is not enough money in the budget or because the town has never provided services for certain disabilities before. All eligible children must be served.

2. EVALUATION. Each child referred for consideration for special education services must be evaluated by a qualified examiner for each suspected disability. The law requires that children be tested fairly to determine if they are eligible for special education. The tests must take into consideration the child's disability and cultural or linguistic background. The evaluation must produce an overall picture of the child, with information on the child's strengths as well as his or her weaknesses.

3. INDIVIDUALIZED EDUCATION PLAN (IEP). Each child receiving special education services must have the services documented in writing. The IEP is the foundation for the child's education and is unique to his or her needs. IDEA requires school systems to provide educational programs designed specifically for each child eligible for special education services.

4. LEAST RESTRICTIVE ENVIRONMENT. Children with disabilities must be educated with their nondisabled peers in community schools to the "maximum extent appropriate." Whenever possible, children receiving special education services should be placed in the school which they would attend if they did not have a disability. Children with disabilities are to be placed in special classes or separate schools "only when the nature and severity of the handicap is such that education in regular classes" is not appropriate to the needs of the child.

5. PARENTS ARE PARTNERS. The law include parents as partners in the planning and decision-making process with regard to the education of their children. It guarantees parental access to records; requires notice to parents of all decision-making meetings; and mandates that written parental consent be obtained before evaluation testing, before initial placement in special education, and before changes in placement.

6. DUE PROCESS. IDEA requires each state to provide legal means for parents and education professionals to have a hearing of their disputes conducted by a qualified, impartial examiner.

Learning More about IDEA

More detail on procedures and your rights under IDEA are in Chapter 6, "Getting Started in Special Education." Information regarding your state's regulations is available from several sources, including the Parent Training and Information Center (PTIC) in your state, and local chapters of the Association for Retarded Citizens (ARC). These groups also provide training and summaries of state regulations, as do other local organizations. Copies of all pertinent documents can be obtained from your state department of education, office of special education.

The Rehabilitation Act of 1973

The Rehabilitation Act of 1973 (Public Law 93–112) authorizes federal funding for training and placement of people with disabilities in full-time, part-time, or supported employment in the competitive job market. The programs and services authorized under the Rehabilitation Act focus on rehabilitation to enable employment and independent living. The act also provides the foundation for educational programs designed for children with disabilities as those children develop from childhood to adulthood. Because Section 504 of the Rehabilitation Act protects the rights of people with disabilities in programs funded with federal money, it ensures access to educational facilities and programs, including colleges and universities using federal funds, as well as local public schools.

Eligibility

The Rehabilitation Act contains several definitions that affect a person's service eligibility. Except for Title IV (which supports the National Council on Disability) and Title V (which makes it a federal violation to discriminate against a person with disabilities), the act defines an *individual with handicaps* as a person who "has a physical or mental disability which for such individual constitutes or results in a substantial handicap to employment and can reasonably be expected to benefit in terms of employability from vocational rehabilitation services."

Except for purposes of Title VII (independent living services), an *individual with severe handicaps* is defined as a person "who has a severe physical or mental disability which seriously limits one or more functional capacities (such as mobility, communication, self-care, self-direction, interpersonal skills, work tolerance, or work skills) in terms of employability"; "whose vocational rehabilitation can be expected to require multiple vocational rehabilitation services over an extended period of time"; and "who has one or more physical or mental disabilities resulting from amputation, arthritis, autism, blindness, burn injury, cancer, cerebral palsy, cystic fibrosis, deafness, head injury, heart disease, hemiplegia, respiratory or pulmonary dysfunction, mental retardation, mental illness, multiple sclerosis, muscular dystrophy, musculoskeletal disorders, neurological disorders (including stroke and epilepsy), paraplegia, quadriplegia, and other spinal cord conditions, sickle cell anemia, specific learning disability, end-state renal disease, or another disability or combination of disabilities determined on the basis of an evaluation of rehabilitation potential to cause comparable substantial functional limitation."

As regards independent living services, an *individual with severe handicaps* is defined as a person "whose ability to function independently in family and community or whose ability to engage or continue in employment is so limited by the severity of his or her physical or mental disability that independent-living rehabilitation services are required in order to achieve a greater level of independence in functioning in family or community or engaging or continuing in employment."

Important Points

Sixteen programs are authorized within the Rehabilitation Act of 1973. Although these programs are defined by the law, not all are funded by Congress in a given year. For example, five of the programs were not funded in fiscal year 1991, and one was only partly funded. Although individual states have their own policies on how and to whom to provide services and on the priority in which individuals are served, the act does require priority be given to the most severely disabled. The selection policies are subject to certain guidelines and approval by the U.S. Department of Education, the federal agency that administers the act.

Through the various programs contained within it, the Rehabilitation Act provides many services. These services may be funded in whole or in part through the act, depending on the financial resources of the person with disabilities. The actual services provided depend on the individual's needs, as defined in the Individual Written Rehabilitation Program (IWRP). On the next page is a list of services that may be included in an IWRP.

The IWRP is written jointly by a rehabilitation counselor and the disabled person (and his or her parent or guardian, if necessary). It contains the terms and conditions under which services will be provided and sets out long-term and intermediate-term goals. IWRPs must be reviewed at least every 12 months.

The Rehabilitation Act protects the rights of each individual receiving services under it. For example, if a person is capable of accomplishing a goal contained in his IWRP, he or she must have the opportunity to do so. Special services are provided to the hearing and visually impaired. For example, all states have either a separate commission or special vocational rehabilitation unit that works only on services for the blind. The Deafness and Communicative Disorders Branch within the Rehabilitation Services Administration works with state agencies to develop rehabilitation services for the deaf and persons with communicative disorders. The National Technical Institute for the Deaf (NTID) is a residential postsecondary training facility. NTID promotes employment of the deaf by providing technical training and education.

The act defines *supported employment* as "competitive work in integrated settings—(a) for individuals with severe handicaps for whom competitive employment has not traditionally occurred; or (b) for individuals for whom competitive employment

Potential IWRP Services

➤ diagnosis and evaluation of rehabilitation potential

➤ counseling, guidance, referral, and placement services

➤ vocational and other training

➤ disabled youth job training

➤ enhancement of employment opportunities: community services, competitive employment, business opportunities, supported employment

➤ transportation to rehabilitation services and place of employment

➤ social and recreational services

➤ independent-living services

➤ health care

➤ mental health services

➤ attendant care

➤ income maintenance

➤ technological aids and devices

➤ interpreter and reader services

➤ services to family members when necessary to meet rehabilitation objectives

➤ services to preschool children

has been interrupted or intermittent as a result of a severe disability, and who, because of their handicap, need ongoing support services to perform such work."

Independent living services grants are available to states and independent not-for-profit organizations to provide appropriate living arrangements for people with disabilities. The living arrangements must be in support of current or future employment, and foster the independence of the individual with disabilities. Independent living arrangements vary from group homes to condominiums owned by the individuals with disabilities, but are supported through the act. This support can take the form of financial assistance or any combination of the services listed above, as a combined service.

Each state must provide information on how to access benefits available under the Rehabilitation Act, as well as advocacy services to ensure the protection of rights under the act. These advocacy services must be provided by an agency separate from the one administering the programs for the state.

The National Council on Disability is funded through the Rehabilitation Act. Council members (appointed by the President and approved by the U.S. Senate) are responsible for reviewing all federal statutes related to persons with disabilities. They must determine the extent to which laws offer opportunities for "independence and community integration." The Council formulates legislative recommendations and proposals for the President and the Congress.

Section 504

Section 504 of the Rehabilitation Act is civil rights legislation enforced by the U.S. Department of Education Office for Civil Rights. According to Section 504, a person is *disabled* if he or she has: "(A) a physical or mental impairment that substantially limits one or more of the major life activities of such individual; (B) a record of such an impairment; or (C) ... [is] regarded as having such an impairment." Major life activities include: breathing, caring for oneself, hearing, learning, seeing, speaking, walking, and working. This is the same definition used in the Americans with Disabilities Act.

Section 504 prohibits discrimination against persons with disabilities in programs funded with federal money. It protects the right of people with disabilities to have equal access to programs and services. It also requires that accommodations be made to allow inclusion. Courts have reinforced this component, finding that accommodations are necessary to allow "meaningful equal opportunity."

Learning More about the Rehabilitation Act

The Office of Special Education and Rehabilitative Services within the U.S. Department of Education is responsible for overall administration of the Rehabilitation Act. It can provide you with summaries of the act and the programs it supports, and can also assist you in locating the appropriate state agency. Local and state special education departments should also be able to provide you with information regarding programs and services. As your child moves from special education to adulthood, planning for rehabilitation services (if appropriate) must be on the agenda of each annual IEP review meeting. Additional information on this important planning can be found in the section on transition planning in Chapter 7.

The U.S. government publication *Accommodating the Spectrum of Individual Abilities** also offers useful information regarding posteducation programs for individuals with disabilities.

Other Legislation Supporting
People with Disabilities

In addition to the laws reviewed above, many other federal statutes support children and adults with disabilities. Four major statutes are discussed below. The list on the next page includes other laws that may also be of help, depending on your family's circumstances.

Americans with Disabilities Act

The Americans with Disabilities Act (ADA) was passed in July 1990. The purpose of the act is fourfold:

- "to provide a clear and comprehensive national mandate for the elimination of discrimination against individuals with disabilities;...

---

* Available from the U.S. Commission on Civil Rights (Clearinghouse Publication #81) .

Other Legislation of Interest

➤ **Access**
Architectural Barriers Removal Act
Urban Mass Transportation Act
Federal-Aid Highway Act
Rail Passenger Service Act
Federal Aviation Act

➤ **Education**
Family Educational Rights and Privacy Act
Education Consolidation and Improvement Act
Education of the Deaf Act of 1986
Helen Keller National Center Act

➤ **Employment**
Job Training Partnership Act
Fair Labor Standards Act
Small Business Act
Wagner-Peyser Act

➤ **Housing**
United States Housing Act of 1937
Housing Act of 1949
National Affordable Housing Act
Fair Housing Act

➤ **Military Personnel and Their Families**
Defense Dependents Education Act of 1978
Military Medical Benefits Act (CHAMPUS)

➤ **Rehabilitation**
Technology Assistance Act
Javits-Wagner-O'Day Act
Randolph-Sheppard Act

➤ **Social Services**
Adoption Assistance
Domestic Volunteer Service Act of 1973
Older Americans Act
Head Start

- to provide clear, strong, consistent, enforceable standards addressing discrimination against individuals with disabilities;...
- to ensure that the federal government plays a central role in enforcing the standards established in this Act on behalf of individuals with disabilities; and...
- to invoke the sweep of congressional authority, including the power to enforce the fourteenth amendment and to regulate commerce, in order to address the major areas of discrimination faced day-to-day by people with disabilities."

The Americans with Disabilities Act is viewed by many as landmark legislation that signaled a positive change in attitudes toward the protection of the rights of people with disabilities in the United States. The act prohibits discriminatory employment practices, prohibits discrimination in public services, protects the rights and privileges of people with disabilities in privately operated settings, and requires the installation of special telecommunication equipment for people with speech and hearing impairments. ADA differs from IDEA and Section 504 of the Rehabilitation Act in that it prohibits discrimination in private as well as public settings. IDEA and Section 504 protect the rights of the disabled only in programs using federal funds.

ADA defines *disability* as "(A) a physical or mental impairment that substantially limits one or more of the major life activities of such individual; (B) a record of such an impairment; or (C) being regarded as having such an impairment." For purposes of employment, a *qualified individual with a disability* is defined by the act as "an individual with a disability who, with or without reasonable accommodation, can perform the essential functions of the employment position."

To learn more about the Americans with Disabilities Act contact one of the federal agencies that administer it: the Equal Employment Opportunities Commission, the U.S. Department of Justice, the U.S. Department of Transportation, and the Federal Communications Commission. (Contact information is provided in Appendix B.)

Developmental Disabilities Assistance and Bill of Rights Act

The Developmental Disabilities Assistance and Bill of Rights Act assists states in developing and implementing comprehensive programs for identifying and meeting the needs of people who are developmentally disabled. The act states that people with developmental disabilities have a right to "appropriate treatment, services, and rehabilitation," in the least restrictive settings that are devised to maximize the person's potential for development and independence.

The act mandates that all programs, including those provided in residential and nonresidential settings, must meet certain minimum standards (defined within the act) to qualify for government funding. The law also provides for a protection and advocacy agency within each state. This agency must be separate from the agency that administers the act.

This federal statute mandates that school facilities be accessible. School systems must make some of their existing buildings handicapped accessible and all new schools must be fully accessible to the disabled. Where complete renovation is not done, your child's classrooms (including homeroom, lunch room, music room, etc.) must be accessible to him or her, even if this requires moving your child's class to the first floor of a multifloor building. It is your child's right under law to have such accommodations made. Access to facilities is also covered by Section 504 of the Rehabilitation Act.

A 1978 amendment to the Developmental Disabilities Assistance Act incorporated a new definition of developmental disability. As defined in the amended act, the term *developmental disability* means "a severe, chronic disability of a person which:

- is attributable to a mental or physical impairment or combination of mental and physical impairment;
- is manifested before the person attains age 22;
- is likely to continue indefinitely;
- results in substantial limitations in three or more of the following areas of major life activity: (a) self-care,

(b) receptive and expressive language, (c) learning, (d) mobility, (e) self-direction, (f) capacity for independent living, and (g) economic self-sufficiency;

- reflects the person's need for a combination of special interdisciplinary or generic care, treatment or other services which are (a) of lifelong or extended duration and (b) individually planned and coordinated."

The U.S. Department of Health and Human Services can provide you with additional information regarding developmental disabilities legislation. (Contact information is provided in Appendix B.)

Social Security Act

The Social Security Act contains four programs affecting people with disabilities: Medicare, Medicaid, Social Security Income (SSI), and Social Security Disability Insurance (SSDI).

Medicare provides health insurance benefits to qualified individuals. Medicaid is the medical assistance program for low-income individuals, including individuals with disabilities. SSI is an income assistance program administered by the federal government, providing direct cash payments to low-income elderly people and to people with disabilities whose income and resources are below specified levels. Eligibility for disabled individuals age 18 or older is based solely on the individual's diagnosis and financial situation; the parents' income and assets are not considered. SSDI is available to individuals with disabilities who have a parent who has participated in Social Security and is entitled to retirement payments, or whose parent has died. Contact the Social Security Administration (listed in Appendix B) for additional information and assistance regarding any of these four programs.

National Library Service for Persons Who Are Blind and Physically Disabled

The National Library Service for Persons Who Are Blind and Physically Disabled provides books, magazines, and musical scores in braille and on recorded media to eligible individuals free of charge. The materials are distributed through a cooperative network of regional and local libraries and through the mail. To be eligible, a person must be unable to read or otherwise use standard printed materials due to temporary or permanent visual impairment. Also, "other physically handicapped readers certified by a competent authority as unable to read normal printed materials as a result of physical limitations" are eligible for services under this law. For example, if appropriately certified, a person with learning disabilities is eligible for services under this act. Contact your local library for additional information.

6 School Systems: Getting Started in Special Education

Schools form the focus of your child's life for many years. They may be the focus because your child hates school, loves school, or simply because he or she spends so much time there. Because you are the parent of a child with a disability, school may be the focal point of your life as well. The school system forms an important specialty team within the larger team supporting you and your child. The school team may include many different players, including teachers, therapists, administrators, and the school support staff. Many of these people will come and go throughout your child's years in school. For this reason, it is important that you be a central player on your child's team. Parents are equal partners in planning educational programs for their children.

This chapter deals with getting started in special education. Chapter 7 concentrates on daily school life after placement and your child's movement to postsecondary education. Some of the events described here are unique to getting started in special education, others will recur throughout the time your child receives services.

A number of people may be members of the formal or informal team that works with your child. The formal team comprises the individuals directly responsible for carrying out the services outlined in your child's Individualized Educational Plan (IEP) and may include a resource room teacher, a speech and language pathologist, a classroom teacher, and others. The informal team includes anyone working or in frequent contact with your child, helping him or her to succeed. Your child's informal team may comprise the principal, the physical education teacher, and your son or daughter's classmates.

The Players

Regardless of your child's needs and the makeup and size of the team, it is likely that you will encounter many new people once you enter the world of special education. Some will become your close allies. Others may become your adversaries. Whenever possible, adversarial relationships should be avoided. Certain professionals may work with your child for one year while others may provide services for four or more years. To make sure that your child receives the best education possible, you must build and maintain strong relationships with all of them. I find it helpful to keep a list posted of the key people on Lara's team (a sample appears on the following page).

Administrators

School administrators, particularly the special education administrator and the principal, play key roles in the lives of children with disabilities and their parents. Building solid relationships with these professionals is fundamental to the success of your child's school experience.

The special education administrator is responsible for all special education programs and authorizes the provision of services to children with disabilities. Special education administrators typically report to the superintendent of schools for a particular school district. Large communities may have more than one special education administrator; small communities may combine special education administration with other responsibilities to form a position often referred to as "director of pupil personnel services." An administrator functioning in this

Sample Key People List

School Administration		*SSS/SSS-SSSS*
Resource Room Teacher:		*Mary Blake*◆
Third Grade Teacher:		*Janice White*◆
Speech & Language Pathologist:		*Michael Shapiro*◆
Occupational Therapist:		*Michelle Chopin*◆
Physical Therapist:		*Diane Martins*◆
Guidance:		*Bob Abels*◆
Principal:		*Dan Reeves*◆
Director of Pupil Personnel Services:		*Susan Dowling*◆
Physicians		
Pediatrician:	*Dr. Moyns*◆	*SSS-7800*
Neurologist:	*Dr. Michaels*◆	*SSS-2100*
Dentist:	*Dr. Koins*◆	*SSS-2900*
Ophthalmologist:	*Dr. Owen*◆	*SSS-0040*

capacity may also be responsible for the English as a Second Language program and for guidance services for the district.

Whatever his or her title, the special education administrator is responsible for the special education budget, for providing appropriate staff development opportunities, for the hiring of the special education staff, and for the coordination of related inservice training. This training is not necessarily for special education staff members only but may include all educators. For example, the special education administrator is responsible for providing education to the general staff regarding special education considerations.

The special education administrator is the public official ultimately responsible for ensuring that the school district follows the applicable state and federal regulations regarding special education and related services, that timelines are maintained, and that all students entitled to special education and related services receive a free and appropriate education in the least restrictive environment possible. Announcements regarding IEP team meetings and evaluations come from the special education administration office.

The principal sets the tone of a school and is responsible for facilitating communication between teachers and parents, teachers and teachers, parents and parents, students and teachers, and students and students. A good principal knows all the students within the building and is often seen talking with teachers, parents, and students. For students mainstreamed into a general classroom, the principal can play a key role in making inclusion successful. Since both general and special education teachers receive direction from the principal, he or she is the perfect candidate for helping to resolve issues involving integration of children with disabilities into the mainstream.

Teachers

Teachers touch the lives of children more than any other professional. The influence teachers have on children with disabilities can be even greater than their influence on typical children. This influence can be positive or negative. For the child whose disability goes undetected, a misguided teacher may think the child is lazy or that problems at home are causing the child to behave inappropriately in school. Or a teacher may be a child's guiding light, opening doors for him or her by adapting to the child's unique learning style.

Over the years, several different types of teachers will work with your child. As schools continue to move toward the inclusion of children with disabilities into general classrooms, and as your child's needs change, the teachers' types and roles will change.

The general classroom teacher is responsible for educating a class of children, all of whom are usually in the same grade. The class may include typical children and those with disabilities. If your child spends time in a general classroom, the classroom teacher will be a member of the IEP team. He or she will be responsible for not only carrying out components of the IEP, but also for helping to develop the IEP. A general classroom teacher can make the difference in your child's ability to interact with his or her peers and be a participating member of the class.

Many students receive services from a "drop-in" resource room teacher. In some schools, the resource teacher "drops in" on the general classroom and provides special education services within the mainstream. The traditional approach, however, is for children to go to the resource room at regularly scheduled times to receive individualized instruction. Some schools combine these two approaches, with the resource room teacher spending time in the general classroom as well as in the resource room.

Some children require more concentrated attention than can be provided in a general classroom or with the assistance of a resource room teacher. These children are often in substantially separate classrooms and participate in the mainstream to varying degrees. These separate classrooms will have different names in different school districts, such as learning centers or primary resource classrooms.

Resource room teachers must have college degrees in special education. Many will have worked in general classrooms as well. The resource room teacher is likely to be the IEP team leader or facilitator. He or she has primary responsibility for ensuring that your child receives the services outlined in the IEP.

Children receiving services from a resource room teacher, either on a drop-in basis or in a self-contained setting, are likely to work with the same teacher for several years. Building a strong relationship with your child's resource room teacher can facilitate communication between you and the school system in general. Working closely with the special education teacher as well as the classroom teacher allows you to share ideas and strategies that promote your child's learning, independence, and self-esteem.

In school systems where students with disabilities are fully included in general classrooms, a number of different setups may be used. Many systems employ integration specialists, responsible for working with classroom teachers on effective strategies and techniques for including children with disabilities in the general classroom. Although in some schools the integration specialist functions as the IEP team leader, the responsibility for the delivery of services detailed in the IEP falls more often on the classroom teacher.

Classrooms that include children with disabilities often have an aide present. Although the aide's primary responsibility involves the education of the students with disabilities, this professional is available to work with all the children in the class. The same holds true in a team teaching model where a general teacher and a special education teacher share responsibility for a class. School systems define the responsibility for carrying out the IEP differently when a team teaching approach is used, however. In some cases it is shared, in others it is the primary responsibility of either the special or general education teacher.

If your child is in a residential placement, his or her team will include special education teachers, therapists, and those responsible for providing daily living assistance. The latter may include a residential counselor and the people who maintain the facility. Whenever a child is placed out of district, a liaison will be established between the placement and the school system.

Therapists

Your child may receive related services from a number of specialists, depending on his or her needs. Chapter 4 provided some suggestions on working effectively with the specialists in your child's life. In the school setting, some additional considerations should be noted.

Over 50% of the children receiving special education services receive speech and language therapy.[*] These services are provided by a speech and language pathologist in a number of possible settings. Therapy may concentrate primarily on speech, on language, or on both, depending on the needs of the student. Your child may work with the speech and language pathologist on an individual basis, in a small group setting, or within the general or resource classroom. Your child's IEP may also outline a combination of these approaches.

---

[*] Mary-Beth Fafard, Associate Commissioner of Special Education in Massachusetts, as stated at the Learning Disabilities Association of Massachusetts annual conference in March, 1993.

Physical therapists may work with your child if he or she needs help with gross motor skills. Physical therapists teach children exercises that may strengthen their large muscles (abdominal muscles, for example, versus finger muscles, which are referred to as small or fine muscles) and improve their coordination. They teach children using wheelchairs or other adaptive equipment how to use the equipment while ensuring that the equipment is fitted properly. Many children who receive physical therapy enjoy their time with the therapist; they view the activities as fun. As with speech and language therapy, physical therapy may be conducted in several ways. Although some schools include physical therapy within the general classroom setting, conducting therapy sessions with one or a few children is most common.

Occupation refers to daily living activities, such as getting dressed or eating. Occupational therapists work with children who have difficulties developing fine motor skills or sensory integration.* Your child may receive occupational therapy in settings similar to those used for physical therapy.

Psychologists, Guidance Counselors, and Social Workers

The school psychologist typically handles evaluations, assessments, and consultations. The school psychologist conducts the psychological component of the evaluation and prepares a written assessment of the testing. Some school psychologists, however, do work directly with students in individual or group therapy settings. Teachers, parents, and students, as well as anyone working in behalf of children within a particular school system, may call upon the school psychologist for assistance.

Guidance counselors and social workers function in similar capacities in schools, particularly at the elementary school

---

* "Sensory experiences include touch, movement, body awareness, sight, sound, and the pull of gravity. The process of the brain organizing and interpreting this information is called sensory integration. Sensory integration provides a crucial foundation for later, more complex learning and behavior." (From *Sensory Integration Information Sheet*, published by Sensory Integration International, 1992.)

level. When children reach high school, a guidance counselor may be responsible for educating and assisting students and parents in regard to college, vocational training, or other post-secondary education options.

Guidance counselors or social workers work with children, typically in group settings, on a number of matters. They may conduct weekly peer communication and relationship-building sessions where students learn social problem-solving skills. Some school systems offer parent training programs as a part of their counseling services. These programs are typically open to all parents, not just parents of children with disabilities. School counselors are also often available to parents and to other school personnel on an as-needed basis. If your child receives services from a school counselor that are detailed in the IEP, the counselor is considered a member of your child's formal team.

Others

If your child takes medication while at school, you will be talking with the school nurse. School nurses are responsible for ensuring that all medication is administered in accordance with state and local regulations. School nurses are often members of the formal team because they usually are the persons who conduct home assessments, a component of the evaluation.

All too often, however, schools do not have a designated full-time nurse. The school secretary frequently plays the role of nurse when the nurse is not in the building. Having the secretary as an ally can help you far beyond the topic of medication.

Cathy, the secretary at my daughter's elementary school, plays a key role in communication. I frequently ask Cathy to relay messages to Lara's teachers and therapists, as well as to the principal.

Your child will undoubtedly encounter many other professionals during his or her years in school. The physical education, art, or music teacher may be a special person in your child's life, either because your child has a special talent or because he or she simply likes the teacher. Encouraging positive relationships between your child and these teachers may create a much-needed outlet for your child.

The Special Education Process

Whether you initiated a screening or referral or someone else did, getting started in the special education process can be overwhelming. You may be dealing with the diagnosis of a disability at the same time as you are going through a process that is foreign to you. Even when the acceptance of your child's diagnosis is behind you, meeting many new people, hearing new words, and going to meetings where professionals are telling you everything that is wrong with your child can be stressful and agonizing.

The first thing to do is to get out your calendar! Mark the dates of evaluations and meetings so that you can be sure events happen according to the timelines required by your state's regulations. Knowing when events are scheduled will also help you and your child to prepare appropriately.

The Individuals with Disabilities Education Act (IDEA) touches the lives of children with disabilities and young adults more than any other federal law. It protects the disabled individual's rights as well as those of the parents and establishes guidelines that must be followed by state and local school departments. It requires school systems to follow specific procedures and timelines to ensure parent participation in the special education process and to protect the rights of the child and the family. It is the foundation upon which all state regulations for special education are based. Knowledge of IDEA, however, does not take the place of knowledge of your state's specific regulations or your local school department's procedures and regulations, as we saw in Chapter 5.

Parental Involvement

IDEA is based on the belief that parents are to be involved in the decision-making process concerning their children's education.

Some states have taken this further in their own regulations than other states. Where your state does not explicitly state that parents must be involved in a particular event, there is no harm in asking to be involved. It is your right as a parent to be involved in your child's education.

The school must notify you, as a parent, of all decision-making meetings once your child is determined to be eligible for special education. This notification must be in writing and must include the meeting date, time, location, purpose, and names of participants. Meetings must be held at times agreeable to parents and the school system. Although IDEA dictates certain timelines, it is important to be familiar with those in your state because they may differ from those in the federal regulations. For example, Rhode Island has reduced the number of days between events in the process. All states are mandated by law to stay within the timelines detailed in IDEA.

IDEA also protects parental access to children's school records. Under the law, you have the right to receive copies of your child's records within two consecutive weekdays of request. Should you find mistakes or misleading information in the file, you may request that the records be amended. To further protect your child, each state has policies securing the confidentiality of records.

Each child receiving special education must have an IEP (Individualized Education Plan). The IEP defines the special education and related services to be delivered to a child with disabilities. Special education is defined in IDEA as "specially designed instruction, at no cost to parents or guardians, to meet the unique needs of a child with a disability, including classroom instruction, instruction in physical education, home instruction and instruction in hospitals and institutions." Related services are defined in IDEA as "transportation, and such developmental, corrective and other supportive services...as may be required to assist a child with a disability to benefit from special education," including transportation, speech and language pathology, audiology, psychotherapy, physical and occupational therapy, recreation, physical education, counseling, medical services, early identification and assessment of disabling conditions in children, parent counseling and training, school health, and vocational education.

First Steps

The IEP is developed and put into place in a process that is defined by IDEA and by your state's special education law. The process includes onetime events as well as events that repeat periodically. The initial steps, often the most overwhelming, have to be endured only once!

The first step in the process is the identification of a problem. For severely disabled children, the existence of a problem is often known at birth. For children with milder disabilities, however, identification of a problem may not occur until the child is well into elementary school or even later. You may be the first person to suspect a problem, or it may be your child's classroom teacher or pediatrician. Once a problem has been recognized, the traditional next step is screening. The screening process is used to determine whether a full evaluation is warranted. After screening, a written referral must be made to the director of special education in order for an evaluation to take place. The evaluation (or testing) phase assesses your child's strengths and weaknesses. Once completed, the evaluation results are reviewed and a determination is made as to whether your child is eligible for special education. If your child is found eligible, the evaluation team will meet with you to develop an education plan for your child. This plan will be documented in the form of an IEP. Before placement in a special education program, you must provide your consent by signing the IEP. After you approve the IEP, your child will be placed in an appropriate education program. Your child's progress will then be reviewed at least once a year. The process, time frames, and decision points are shown in more detail on the next two pages.

Screening

The screening process is used to determine if a complete evaluation of your child should be conducted. Parents or others within the school system may request a screening. If you choose

Special Education Process Overview

Step	Decision	Decision Maker	IDEA Timeframe
Problem Identification	Is action needed?	Varies	
Screening Request			
Screening			Within 30 days of Screening Request
Screening Review Meeting	Perform evaluation?	School system	
Referral for evaluation	What areas should be evaluated?	School System	
Evaluation Consent	Should child be tested?	Parent	
Pre-evaluation			

Step	Purpose/Question	Responsible	Timeline
Conference Evaluation			Within 45 days of Screening and 30 days of Consent
Eligibility Meeting	Child eligible?	School system	Within 30 days of Evaluation
IEP Development Meeting	Appropriate setting and specific services with associated goals and objectives.	Team (parents and school system representatives)	Within 30 days of Eligibility Meeting
IEP Development			
IEP Approval	Meet needs of my child?	Parent	
Placement			
Annual Review	Is child achieving goals and objectives?	Team	Every 12 months
Reevaluation	What areas should be evaluated?	School System	Every three years

to request a screening, do so in writing to the special education administrator for your local school system. If someone within the school system recommends that a child be screened, federal law does not require parental notification. Some states, however, do require communication of the results to parents.

Some school systems require parental attendance at screening meetings, most allow it when asked. It is best if you participate in the screening review meeting, at which the decision will be made regarding an evaluation. If you are unable to attend the meeting due to the school's resistance, review the results carefully with the classroom teacher or principal.

Children must be screened within 30 days of a request. The screening committee (often referred to as a local school screening committee, education management team, child study committee, or school-based committee) is responsible for reviewing the child's strengths and weaknesses and discussing possible classroom alterations and accommodations. These committees usually comprise the principal, the person who made the request, teachers, and specialists. The committee may decide to implement some classroom modifications before referring your child for a complete evaluation and reconvene afterward to determine if the modifications were successful. The committee may also decide that no alterations are necessary and an evaluation is not warranted. Referring your child for a comprehensive evaluation is the last option (see the section on "Referral").

The committee's decision must be sent in writing to the special education administrator. Your local school system procedures and regulations will outline the time requirements. If you disagree with the committee's decision, you may challenge it, an option discussed later in this chapter under "Due Process."

If the decision is to make classroom modifications and not proceed with an evaluation, be certain you know what accommodations are to be made. Staying in close contact with the classroom teacher in this circumstance enables you to determine if the correct decision was made. Schedule weekly phone calls or request weekly progress reports with your child's teacher. Also convene a meeting approximately one month after the modifications are implemented.

Referral

While anyone can refer a child for a special education evaluation, it is typically a screening committee or parent that takes this action. If the screening committee determines that your child should have a complete evaluation, a referral will be made in writing to the local special education administrator. If the disability is obvious, as with a child who is blind or has Down syndrome, the screening may be skipped and the process will begin with a referral. When no screening is necessary, a referral may come directly from you or your child's physician (a sample referral letter appears on the next page). Some states allow anyone to make a referral, but if the referral comes from outside the school system, an evaluation must take place. Regardless of the source, referrals must be in writing to the local special education administrator.

Evaluation

The special education administrator must receive your consent in writing before an evaluation of your child can begin. The notice informing you that your child has been referred for an evaluation should include a list of the assessments to be conducted. Assessments may evaluate your child's educational history, current educational performance, medical/health history, and home setting, and his or her psychological, speech and language, occupational therapy, and physical therapy needs. If you believe that additional assessments should be performed, you have the right to request them. As a parent, you also have the right to request that outside specialists working with your child be members of the evaluation team. If your child's case is complex, or if you have a disagreement over what areas should be tested, consider including the special education administrator in this conference.

The objective of the evaluation is to assess your child's strengths and weaknesses and determine if he or she is eligible for special education services. Many parents find it helps to meet with the person heading up the evaluation team (often referred to as the team leader or case manager) for a preassessment conference. A preassessment conference gives you the

---

Sample Referral Letter (from Parent)

September 1, 1986

Director of Special Education
Forest Avenue
Anycity, USA 00000

Dear Director:

My daughter Lara will turn three on October 19, 1986 and should be evaluated to determine if she is eligible for special education or related services. Lara has been delayed in achieving her developmental milestones since birth. She has been receiving speech and language therapy twice a week for six months. I have consulted with Lara's pediatrician as well as her neurologist, and we all feel strongly that Lara needs to be in a language-based preschool program.

Thank you and I look forward to hearing from you.

Sincerely,

Lizanne Capper
123 Main Street
Anycity, USA 00000
555/555-5555

---

opportunity to learn more about the different types of tests that are planned for your child. The team leader should be able to give you not only a schedule of the assessments but also to describe the testing process itself. For example, the team leader should be able to tell you how long your child will be with each evaluator and what tests will be conducted. A psychological evaluation typically includes a test to measure intelligence, for example. There are four different types of IQ tests commonly used (Bayley Scales, Leiter, Stanford-Binet Scale, and Wechsler Scales), with variations of each depending on the age of the child. If your child has a significant communication disorder, it is critical that an IQ test be used that relies on nonverbal reasoning abilities. Leiter, WISC-R, and Stanford-Binet are potential candidates in this case. Regardless of the area being tested, the assessment team is required by law to use tests that take your child's disability into account.

When reviewing the schedule of assessments, be certain that your child will be tested during his "good periods." If your child is not a morning person, conducting a test at 8:30 A.M. is not likely to give the evaluator a true picture of your child's abilities. Conversely, your child may tire more easily in the afternoon and therefore morning may be the best time for testing. If a test is scheduled at a time that is inappropriate for your child, ask that it be rescheduled. This is your right under federal law. All testing must be nondiscriminatory; evaluations should provide an accurate assessment of your child's strengths and weaknesses.

Preparing your child for an evaluation is very likely your most important role in the evaluation phase after giving consent for the evaluation. Your child's age is a factor that must obviously be taken into consideration, but he or she must understand the process as much as possible. Before the evaluation begins, you may want to explain what and why he or she will be going through over the next several weeks. And the morning of each test, remind your child of what will be happening that day. Follow up with your child or the teacher at the end of each day a testing session is scheduled to be certain it took place and to find out how it went.

If your child is not feeling well on a day when testing is to take place, or if there is some other reason that your child would not perform at his or her usual level, consider having the session rescheduled. You may want to discuss this with the team leader or classroom teacher and reach a joint decision. In any event, the team leader should be notified of any significant events during the course of the evaluation. This will help the team members as they develop their final assessments. Some parents find it useful to keep a diary during the time period and to share it with the team once the testing concludes but before the assessments are written. Entries to this diary may include the mood your child is in each day and any events that were out of the ordinary.

Under IDEA, the evaluation must be completed within 45 days of screening and within 30 days after you give your consent for testing. Should you disagree with the outcome of the evaluation, you have the right to request an independent evaluation at public expense. The section later in this chapter on "Due Process" provides further information.

Reevaluations of children in special education programs are required at least every three years. Younger children are sometimes reevaluated more frequently. As with the initial evaluation, parental consent is required before testing. Parents also have the right to request a reevaluation at any time. If the school system disagrees, due process may be invoked.

Eligibility

After the evaluation is completed, the team leader will convene an eligibility meeting to determine whether your child will receive special education services. In cases where eligibility is straightforward, the eligibility meeting may be combined with the IEP development meeting discussed below. Should an eligibility meeting be required, it must take place within 30 days of the completion of the evaluation. When it is combined with the IEP development meeting, the dual-purpose session must take place within 30 days of the last day of testing.

Some school systems include parents in eligibility meetings; others do not. If not explicitly invited, you should request your inclusion. Your attendance is critical if there is any question on the part of the school system as to whether your child is eligible for services. Parental attendance and participation can play a key role in the decision-making. Not only will you be there to hear the discussion, but you will be able to ask questions and, most importantly, provide insights into your child's needs and abilities. Consider preparing your position ahead of time, as described below in "Preparing for the IEP Planning Meeting."

Preparing for the IEP Planning Meeting

Preparing for your first IEP planning meeting (often referred to as an IEP team meeting), can be overwhelming. You are not sure what to expect or what the outcome will be. You will also be meeting with people you do not know.

First, take comfort in the reality that you already know the most important person—your child. Your role in the IEP development process is to be your child's advocate and the expert on him or her.

The checklist on the next page is to help you prepare for the IEP development meeting. If you can do only one thing in preparation for the meeting, however, make it getting someone to go with you. Do not attend an IEP team meeting alone! Your co-parent, a family member, a friend or an advocate should attend the meeting with you. Not only can this person be a source of emotional support, he or she can be another set of eyes, ears, and hands.

From an advocacy point of view, you will want to make sure your child has been evaluated fairly and that the special education and related services are designed to meet his or her unique needs. You will also want to be assured that the school system is following the state special education regulations.

When the IEP development meeting is scheduled, you will be notified in writing. Review the letter and be sure that the right persons are scheduled to attend the meeting. The special education administrator, or an authorized delegate, must attend the first IEP development meeting and any other team meetings at which decisions regarding placement will be made. Your child's classroom teacher, if applicable, should be in attendance. Some school districts invite the entire evaluation team; others do not. IDEA requires only that someone knowledgeable about the tests used and the actual evaluation performed be in attendance at the IEP development meeting. The evaluation team usually includes a special education teacher, school nurse, school psychologist, and any therapists who have tested your child. If your child is to be mainstreamed into general education activities, the principal and classroom teacher should also attend the meeting. You may want the principal there regardless of the anticipated placement. You have the right to request that specific school system personnel attend team meetings, so do not hesitate to ask.

IEP Development Meeting Preparation Checklist

1. Schedule the IEP development meeting on a date and at a time mutually convenient to you and the school system.
2. Plan for someone to attend the meeting with you.
3. Request that outside professionals working with your child prepare written assessments and attend team meetings, if desired.
4. Receive notice in writing of the scheduled meeting,
5. Confirm your attendance in writing, including comments and requests regarding assessment reports and people who will be attending. (A sample confirmation letter appears on the next page.)
6. Schedule a preparation meeting with the team leader, if desired.
7. Schedule planning session(s) with your co-parent. (See Chapter 2.)
8. Develop one-year, three-year, and age 22 plans for your child. (See Chapter 1.)
9. Review the evaluation assessment reports and develop questions and comments, if applicable.
10. Develop a list of your child's needs and then set priorities.
11. Prepare a list of questions and agenda items for the meeting. Review your lists with your co-parent.

Upon receiving a team meeting notice, you should respond in writing to the special education administrator. In this letter (a sample is on the facing page), you can confirm your attendance as well as those who will be attending with you. You should also list the people within the school system whom you expect to attend. If the IEP team meeting will follow an evaluation of your child, request copies of the assessment reports be available to you at least two days prior to the meeting (this right may vary by state). In your letter, you might also discuss your thoughts for your child in terms of the upcoming academic year and let the

Sample Team Meeting Confirmation Letter

April 12, 1994

Director of Special Education
Forest Avenue
Anycity, USA 00000

Dear Director:

I am writing to confirm Lara's father's and my attendance at the team meeting for her, scheduled for May 15 at 8:00 A.M. We would like the building principal, the secondary resource room teacher, and Lara's third grade teacher in attendance, in addition to the existing team. Also, we would like copies of all assessment reports at least two days prior to the meeting.

Thank you and I look forward to hearing from you.

Sincerely,

Lizanne Capper
123 Main Street
Anycity, USA 00000
555/555-5555

cc: Team Member
      Principal
      Secondary Resource Room Teacher
      Third Grade Teacher

team know if you will be providing any written materials at least two days before the team meeting. Finally, send a copy of your letter to all the people mentioned in it.

As the expert on your child, it is your responsibility to communicate your perspective on your child's needs. This can be done in a number of ways, both orally and in writing. Many parents and educators find it helpful to have parents develop plans for their children. (Ideas and suggestions for the content and the development of these plans are discussed in Chapter 1.)

Some state regulations require that evaluation assessments (the written summary of the testing conducted, prepared by the evaluator) be available to parents before the IEP team meeting. The advantages of having the opportunity to read and digest the reports before the meeting cannot be underscored enough. Even if your state does not require that these reports be available to you before the IEP development meeting, request it in writing when you give your consent for the initial evaluation.

If your school district is not required to and is unwilling to provide the reports in advance of the meeting, try to negotiate to see copies of them at least one hour before the meeting. Simply state that you would like to be as prepared as possible for the meeting and you believe it is in your child's best interest that you have an opportunity to review the reports prior to the meeting. Your school system is likely to comply with reasonable requests.

If you are able to read the evaluation assessments ahead of time, prepare questions and comments on each area tested. The report should be written so that you can understand it, though you may have to look up a few terms or ask someone knowledgeable in the field to interpret portions of the report. The assessment report should give a general description of how to address your child's particular need (e.g., in a physical therapy report, the therapist may recommend that your child receive services for one hour per week). After reviewing a particular report, you should have a comprehensive picture of your child's strengths and weaknesses in the area tested.

When your child is being seen by a therapist outside the school system, request that he or she provide a written assessment of your child's progress to date as well as a description of successful therapeutic approaches. You may also want to consider including in the meeting those outside professionals who have worked with your child. They are all part of your child's team.

Based on your own observations and knowledge of your child's needs, as well as the evaluators' assessments, formulate a set of priorities before the meeting to be certain that the goals and objectives developed during and following the meeting address these needs. You may want to review and modify these priorities after the IEP development meeting, accounting for new information.

> *Janice,♦ a professional advocate and mother of three children with disabilities, believes this preparation puts you in a position of authority and power. Educators are likely to take your opinions more seriously when you are well prepared for an IEP development meeting.*

Finally, develop for the meeting a list of questions and agenda items. Some parents share this list with the team leader before the meeting, but many do not. If you think it will help the progress of the meeting, give a copy of the questions and points you want covered to the team leader a day or so before the meeting is to take place. You may also want to have a preparation meeting with the team leader to review the purpose and agenda for the meeting.

Be prepared for areas of disagreement at the team meeting. Anticipating issues that may arise allows you to decide on which points you are willing to negotiate, and which ones you consider nonnegotiable. If you do not consider yourself a skilled or experienced negotiator, several books are available that describe how to work with others to achieve a win-win outcome. In other words, unlike a sporting event, where someone has to lose, you and the educators are all on the same team—one team working for the advantage of your child.

The IEP Development Meeting

The IEP development meeting must take place within 30 days of determination that your child is eligible for special education services. This meeting reviews the evaluation results and determines the framework of the IEP. A representative of the special education department, authorized to commit to the provision of special education and related services for your child, must attend the IEP development meeting. In addition to this representative, teachers, evaluators, the principal, you and your co-parent, and your child (if age 14 or over) may attend the meeting. At a minimum, the special education representative, your child's teacher, and a member of the evaluation team must be present. If the special education representative, teacher, or some other person at the meeting is knowledgeable about the evaluation procedures and is familiar with the evaluation results, an evaluation team member is not required to attend the meeting.* IEP team meetings can include up to a dozen persons or more, and often last over one hour and many times two or more hours. If your child's situation is complex, two or more meetings may be needed for the development of the first IEP.

As prepared as you may feel when you walk into your first IEP team meeting, in all likelihood the experience will be overwhelming. For that reason alone, it is important that you prepare for the meeting and attend it with someone you trust. You have the right to have anyone else attend the meeting, including outside professionals, a friend, a family member, or an advocate.

Be sure to arrive promptly at the meeting and get a good seat (meetings are often held in rooms with child-size chairs!). You may want to bring examples of artwork or schoolwork done by your child or photos of your child and your family. These help remind team members that a child is behind everything that is happening and also offer them an opportunity to see your child from a new perspective. Spreading these items out on the table before the meeting starts can serve as an icebreaker and ease a bit of the tension typically prevalent at initial team meetings.

The purpose of the first IEP development meeting is to:

1. Review the assessment results, giving the team an opportunity to learn from each evaluator his or her findings and recommendations;

2. Determine the appropriate placement for your child and what specific services your child will receive (eligibility should already have been determined); and

3. Develop the framework of the IEP.

---

* Although IDEA does not require it, many parents are more comfortable hearing the evaluation results from the person who performed the assessment. This allows for a comprehensive dialogue about the testing, as well as the evaluator's recommendations.

IEP team meetings usually begin with the team leader making introductions and stating the purpose of the meeting. As persons are introduced, you may want to put a check by their names on your own list of whom you expected to be at the meeting.

Those attending the IEP meeting are typically asked to sign a paper recording their attendance. Your signature on this document only records your attendance; it does not imply your consent to any IEP developed at the meeting. You must have the opportunity afterward to review the results of the IEP development meeting and approve or disapprove the proposed placement at that time. Although many school districts automatically provide copies of the IEP to parents, they are not required to do so by IDEA. If your state regulations do not include this provision, make it known at the beginning of the meeting that you want a copy of the IEP as soon as it is completed.

During the course of the meeting, each specialist will review the findings of his or her evaluation component, or someone knowledgeable about the component will provide this information. The members of the team, including you as a parent, can ask questions or discuss their observations and opinions. If you reviewed the assessment reports before the meeting, make sure your questions are answered before moving on to the next report. If you were not given the opportunity to review the assessments in advance, ask for a few minutes to read the report before the evaluator begins discussing it.

As you listen to the evaluators describe your child, you may feel like crying. Go right ahead. Although evaluations are supposed to focus on abilities as well as disabilities, the tendency at team meetings is to focus on the weaknesses. You may also be surprised during the discussion on placement when the recommendation differs (for better or worse) from your expectations.

At the team meeting at the end of Lara's year in first grade (our fifth team meeting), I cried when the recommendation was made for my daughter to repeat the grade, in spite of my having suggested it as an option a month or so earlier. And there was no way to hide my tears, they came gushing out. Fortunately, Lara's team is sensitive. Someone handed me a box of tissues and her special education teacher suggested that we break for a few minutes.

My friend Cyndy, a professional advocate whose son has been in special education for many years, is quite a savvy lady. Even she cries from time to time at IEP team meetings because, "It's my son we're talking about. And that's very different—it can evoke a lot of emotions!"

Throughout the session it is important that the discussion remain focused on the matters at hand. If the meeting starts to get out of control, ask a direct question aimed at getting things back on track. In general, do not hesitate to ask questions. If you do not understand jargon that is being used, ask that it be restated in terms you can understand. If you do not understand someone's point of view, get a clarification. It is crucial to be assertive (while not being aggressive or combative).

Your child's first IEP development meeting should conclude with a decision regarding placement and an agreement on the framework of the IEP. Placement, described more fully in the following section, refers to the setting in which your child will receive special education and related services. The framework of the IEP includes the specific special education and related services your child will receive, and the major goals of each. You should know upon leaving the team meeting, for example, what therapies your child will receive, and how much, how often, and where. For example, your child may receive speech and language therapy two times per week, 30 minutes each, in a small group with peers. And your child may also get academic assistance in reading five times per week, 20 minutes per session, in a resource room. The guiding principle for placement is that the placement should offer an appropriate education in the least restrictive environment possible.

Near the end of the meeting, review your list of questions and agenda items to make sure that all your interests were covered. If you are unclear or uncomfortable about a particular assessment, request a follow-up meeting with the evaluator. You have the right to ask that the meeting be adjourned and reconvened at any time. This is particularly important if the evaluator is not present at the meeting. Confirm with the team leader when you should expect to receive the IEP for your review. States differ on how approval of placement is obtained. Some require that the IEP itself be signed; others request that parents sign a separate document. Whichever the case in your state, you should not be pressured to document your approval of the IEP at a team meeting. If you are put into this situation, simply state that it is your right to take time to review the results of the meeting and respond to the special education administrator regarding your decision. Finally, thank everyone for their time and let them know that you are looking forward to working with them.

The IEP

The Individualized Education Plan (IEP) is a written document setting forth the 12-month educational plan for your child. It describes your child, the services your child is to receive, and the goals and objectives of those services. In some cases it may be appropriate to have an IEP cover a shorter period of time, as with a very young child or with a child just entering a special education program. In all cases, however, the IEP can not extend for more than a period of 12 months. IDEA requires an annual review of each IEP.

The most important word in IEP is *individualized*. The concept of uniquely designed programs to meet the needs of children and young adults with disabilities is reinforced throughout IDEA. It has also been reinforced by the U.S. Supreme Court in a decision discussed later in this chapter.

The IEP specifies the unique educational program for your child based on his or her disabilities, including the provision of special education and related services. Your child's IEP must include five components, as outlined in IDEA:

STATEMENT OF CURRENT EDUCATIONAL PERFORMANCE LEVELS
This section includes a narrative description of your child and his or her disabilities. It should include statements regarding strengths, weaknesses, and learning style, and should provide a

high-level summary of the evaluation results. It may include IQ test scores.

STATEMENT OF ANNUAL GOALS AND SHORT-TERM INSTRUCTIONAL OBJECTIVES

Goals and objectives for your child should be divided by area of need. For example, if it is determined that your child should receive physical therapy as well as speech and language therapy, there should be separate goals and objectives for physical therapy and for speech and language therapy. The goals should be achievable in 12 months or less. For each goal there must be a set of short-term objectives, designed to ensure progress toward meeting the goal. The objectives should give an indication of the present level of performance, as well as describe in concrete terms what your child must achieve to meet them.

DESCRIPTION OF SPECIFIC SPECIAL EDUCATION AND RELATED SERVICES TO BE PROVIDED

This component describes the special education placement as well as the related services. There should also be a written statement defining the extent to which your child will participate in general (i.e., regular) education programs, including classroom time, physical education, lunch, and other activities. In addition to the protections provided under IDEA, Section 504 of the Rehabilitation Act requires that the general education program make the necessary accommodations to include your child, when appropriate.

Your child's placement should be based on a balance between the least restrictive environment and appropriate education provisions. (The types of special education programs and the impact of mainstreaming were discussed earlier in this chapter). Related services to be provided to your child should be included in this section of the IEP, including the amount of time and the frequency (for example, psychological therapy for 30 minutes twice a week).

PLANNED START DATE AND DURATION OF SERVICES

This component indicates the period of time over which specific services will be provided to your child. This can be 12 or fewer months. In most cases, the services will be provided during the course of the school year. In some cases, services, in whole or in part, may be required over the summer to protect your child against experiencing substantial regression.

APPROPRIATE OBJECTIVE CRITERIA, EVALUATION PROCEDURES, AND SCHEDULES
This component indicates the criteria to be used in determining whether your child is achieving the objectives detailed in his or her IEP. The determination must be made at least once a year. The criteria should be written in such a way that they are objective and clear to the entire team working with your child, including you. They must clearly and specifically state what your child must achieve to satisfy each objective.

IEPs are to be developed by your child's team based on the evaluations and the team meeting discussion. The IEP is not written before the meeting because the meeting produces valuable discussion regarding educational alternatives, encompassing your child as a whole.

If your child has difficulties in socialization, a set of goals and objectives should be aimed at improving your child's social problem-solving and relationship-building skills. These may be constructed in such a way that they are the primary responsibility of the classroom teacher, special education teacher, guidance counselor, or some other team member. In many cases it is most effective if the entire team has some responsibilities in a particular focus. Approaches such as Circle of Friends (a group problem-solving technique for inclusion that facilitates input from the child's family, friends, neighbors, classmates, and educators) can be used in this area and if planned, should be documented in the IEP. Many parents and educators find it helpful to conduct the Circle of Friends session before the development of the IEP. If you would like a Circle of Friends session to be considered, discuss it with the team leader during the evaluation process so that a decision can be reached and plans made in concert with the IEP development timelines.

Most state regulations do not require the setting of general classroom objectives if the special education and related services are provided in a pullout fashion, where the child is not mainstreamed. If your child will spend time in a general classroom, however, goals and objectives can be crucial to your child's success in the mainstream. The following are examples of inclusion objectives:

1. *Lara will actively participate in general classroom discussions, progressing beyond active listening and attentiveness (which she achieved in second grade) to contributing personal experiences and opinions.*

2. *Lara will complete academic assignments from the special education teacher in the general classroom at least once a week in the fall, twice a week in the winter, and three times per week in the spring.*

Setting goals for the general education classroom is of particular importance if your child is in a substantially separate classroom and mainstreamed to a certain degree. Children with disabilities must feel they are a part of their general class, because it is crucial for their development of peer relationships and for their self-esteem.

Approval of the IEP

Since the IEP outlines the services your child will receive over 12 months, it is a critical document. You should review it carefully before you approve it, using your notes from the team meeting and the assessment reports as points of reference. Share it with a family member, friend, advocate, or pediatrician or other professionals working with your child. Most importantly, schedule time to go over it with your co-parent.

While it is important to review the document thoroughly, it is equally important to do so within the time frames outlined in your state's regulations. Work with the special education administrator or team leader to modify and clarify points within the IEP. It helps to make these requests in writing promptly after receiving the document. Your child cannot start receiving services until placement is approved.* Children age 18 or older must also approve their own placement.

---

* An exception may be made when a child moves to a new state. The new school district may provide services according to an existing IEP until a new one is developed.

Upon completing your review of the IEP you have four options:

1. Accept the educational program in full;

2. Postpone a decision until the completion of an independent evaluation;

3. Reject the educational program in full; or

4. Reject portions of the educational program, with the understanding that the portions accepted will be implemented immediately.

You are entitled to request an outside evaluation if you select any option other than full acceptance. Before deciding to reject an educational program, consider the alternatives carefully. At this point it is wise to consider hiring a professional advocate (see Chapter 3) to assist in negotiating with the school system so that your child may benefit as much a possible from his or her education.

Placement

There are many types of special education programs. The type your child is placed in should depend on your child's age and unique needs. Many special education programs include some level of mainstreaming, which allows for a continuum of services from special schools to general education classes.

Particular special education placement will differ from one child to another. The services your child receives defines his or her placement, as does the combination of related services provided. A child with an articulation disorder may require speech therapy two times per week, while a child with profound mental retardation and physical disabilities may require intense physical therapy, occupational therapy, and speech and language therapy. Children with learning disabilities may receive the same therapies as children with profound disabilities, but their goals and objectives may be vastly different.

The ideal special education program will be challenging to your child as well as supportive. It will push your child to grow academically as well as socially. The teaching and therapy approaches used should be based on your child's intellectual functioning and communication skills rather than his or her specific disability. Your child's educational program should be designed around the whole child, taking his or her disabilities as well as his or her abilities into consideration. Your child's abilities are the key to his or her success and the combination of these abilities with the disabilities are what makes for a unique program. Educators must draw upon your child's abilities and relative strengths to achieve academic and social success.

Early intervention programs typically focus on the development of communication and social interaction skills. Some programs are made up entirely of children with disabilities, others are integrated with children from the general population. Many school districts offer integrated preschools within a community school. Head Start is one preschool mainstream option as 10% of its students must be children with disabilities.

As noted earlier in this chapter, children may receive special education and related services in a fully included model, in a pullout model, in a substantially separate classroom, in a special school, or in a residential placement. For example, 16,000 local public school districts nationwide serve deaf and hearing-impaired children, but there are also 62 residential schools for deaf children. The right program for your child depends on his or her combination of disabilities as well as intellectual and communication abilities and compensating strengths. The goal is to place children in the least restrictive environment to the greatest extent possible while also providing an appropriate education.

In some situations, the right placement for your child will be clear and straightforward. In other instances, you and the educational agencies with whom you will be working will have to search for the right program. An appropriate placement one year may become inappropriate the next, either because your child is progressing and can move to a less restrictive setting, or because he or she has outgrown the current placement.

Before making any decision regarding placement you should visit all prospective programs. Plan ahead and ask the teacher or appropriate administrator when you can visit his or her program; be sure to explain your child's needs to prospective teachers and other educators.

Janice,♦ the mother of an autistic son, used a preschool checklist as a guide for developing her visit checklist.

Decisions regarding placement can be difficult, especially when the recommended placement is outside of your local school district. You will have to rely on teachers and administrators to put you in touch with other parents whose children are in the program, because these parents can be valuable sources of information. You may also face having to choose whether your child should be in a residential placement. This can be an extremely emotional decision and may call upon you to face issues that you have long kept hidden. If a placement away from home, however, will best ensure your child's chances for a happy, productive, and independent life, it is the right decision for you and your child.

Due Process

IDEA mandates that each state have an appeals process that allows parents to have their disputes heard and decided by an impartial, qualified party. Parents can invoke due process when they: disagree about (1) identification (whether a child is eligible or ineligible for services), (2) evaluation components, (3) evaluation results, (4) placement, or (5) delivery of services.

If you disagree with the evaluation components or results and prevail in due process, you have a right to have your child evaluated independently at public expense. Opting for due process is not always required in order to have the school system pay for an independent evaluation, however. Due process should be used as a last resort after negotiation has failed. Mediation versus a formal hearing should also be considered.

Parents or the school system must request a hearing in writing to invoke due process. Hearings are held much like traditional court cases, including the sharing of documents and witness lists prior to the hearing, and questioning and cross-examination of witnesses. The hearing officer(s) must render a decision in writing.

Each state must provide protection and advocacy services, available at no or low cost to parents in due process procedures. Your local school district is required to provide the necessary information upon request. IDEA also authorizes courts to allow parents to recover attorney's fees when they prevail in court cases under IDEA or other antidiscrimination statutes (such as Section 504 of the Rehabilitation Act or the Americans with Disabilities Act).

U.S. Supreme Court Decisions

The U.S. Supreme Court has issued two decisions of note with regard to special education. The first case, decided in 1982, reinforces several important points concerning "appropriate education" and the requirement that IEPs be designed to meet the specific needs of a child with disabilities.

In *Rowley v. The Board of Education*, the term *appropriate education* was clarified to mean the provision of individualized education and services that aim at more than "minimal academic achievement," The Court, however, decided that "appropriate education" does not require services designed to "maximize a child's potential." Specifically, the IEP should be "reasonably calculated to enable the child to achieve passing marks and advance from grade to grade." The goals must be attainable and the program must meet the standard of "reasonable benefit." Some states have elected to go beyond IDEA and the Supreme Court's interpretation of the act. For example, Massachusetts requires "maximum possible development in a least restrictive environment consistent with students' special needs."

The 1984 Supreme Court ruling in *Irving Independent School District v. Tatro* found that school systems have the responsibility to arrange for the services of a health care professional if the services will enable children to attend their neighborhood school.

7 School Systems: After the Initiation

Getting your child into special education is like pregnancy—it is only the beginning. Making sure that your child receives the education he or she needs and is entitled to takes dedication and diligence. If you had to battle to get your child services in the beginning, it is likely that you will encounter future battles. If getting started in special education was relatively painless, however, you may be taken by surprise when you discover the continual care your child's education requires.

Annual Team Meetings and IEP Updates

As compared to the parents of children in general education, parents of children in special education attend more meetings on behalf of their children; their day-to-day interactions with teachers and specialists are typically more frequent; and they must give more attention to transition planning when their children move to a new school or new teachers, or to postsecondary school life.

In addition to the standard parent-teacher conferences, annual team meetings are conducted for each child receiving special education services. These annual meetings are every bit as important as the initial meetings, and time and energy must be dedicated to preparing for them. As we saw in Chapter 6, the purpose of the annual team meeting is to develop your child's IEP. In many states, new IEPs are developed only upon a full evaluation; in these instances, the purpose of the annual team meeting is to revise the IEP based on your child's current performance and the team's expectations for development over the next 12 months.

Another important objective of the annual team meeting is to give the team, and particularly you as a parent, an opportunity to thoroughly review your child's achievements to date. The meeting should be a constructive dialogue about your child's progress, strengths, weaknesses, and effective teaching strategies. All participants should walk away from the meeting with a better understanding of what makes your child tick!

If your child is integrated with a general education classroom, even if for only brief periods each day, the general education teacher as well as the special education teacher should attend team meetings. The school principal—a critical player in successful inclusion—should participate, as should specialists working with your child, whether within or outside of the school system. In complex cases or where disagreement is anticipated, the special education administrator should attend. Remember, you have the right to have anyone you choose attend team meetings.

When you receive notification of the team meeting, decide whom you want to be there. I confirm my attendance to team meetings with a letter to the special education administrator, documenting whom I expect to be in attendance. I send a copy to each of the people referenced, often followed up by a phone call. (A sample letter appears in Chapter 6.)

Unfortunately, some school systems send team meeting notices home with children instead of mailing them. Although IDEA requires that team meetings be scheduled at mutually convenient times, some parents inevitably miss notices transmitted this way, and because their school system does not adhere closely to the law, may find that the meeting was held without them. This is a clear violation of IDEA. Should this happen to you, you have every right to have the team meeting reconvened. If your school system does not use the mail for team meeting notifications, campaign with other parents to get the procedure changed.

In addition to providing a review of your child's school performance for the past year and a chance to develop or revise the IEP for the next 12 months, the annual team meeting is an opportunity to review your child's placement. Specialists may recommend dropping a service or adding a new one. Particularly when termination of a service is being considered, you should be in agreement and comfortable with any decision to change services. In many cases where it is suspected that a child no longer needs a particular service, establishing a "monitor" phase is beneficial. Although defined differently by each state, this transition service allows the specialist to observe the child for specified time periods before the service is curtailed. This observation period allows for the making of a well-founded decision. In many cases, a reevaluation in the particular area (i.e., occupational therapy) should be conducted before a final decision is made. This allows the specialist and the entire team to compare your child's performance to a standard as well as to previous test results. A team meeting should be held at the end of the monitor time period to make a final determination.

Once you receive a copy of the IEP following an annual team meeting, you should review it thoroughly and compare it to your child's previous IEPs. The suggestions made in the previous chapter regarding the initial IEP also apply to subsequent IEPs.

Reevaluations

Every three years, your child will be reevaluated. Reevaluations may take place more frequently if requested by the parents, or recommended by the school system and agreed to by the parents. Reevaluations typically include the same components as the initial evaluation, although in some circumstances, a component will be added or removed. For example, a child who did not initially exhibit difficulty in gross motor skills may be evaluated by a physical therapist. Conversely, a child who outgrows the need for a particular service, such as occupational therapy, may at some point no longer be tested by an occupational therapist.

Day-to-Day Involvement

Once your child is placed in special education, you may think the hard work is behind you. Unfortunately, your work has only just begun. As a special education administrator stated at a conference I attended, parents cannot take on the "Greyhound bus attitude and leave the driving to the schools." Parents of children with disabilities must be actively involved in their children's education to make certain that things run smoothly. The more services your child receives, the more likely your involvement will increase.

After the initial placement or when there is a change in placement, it is important to get to know the teachers and therapists working with your son or daughter. This can be accomplished in a number of ways and will improve the quality and quantity of communication.

I have found that having my daughter's teachers over to dinner is a good way to get to know them better. This also gives Lara's teachers the opportunity to see her in her home setting where she tends to be more talkative. Visiting over dinner is also less stressful than team meetings and conferences.

Frequent phone conversations and chats before and after school also help keep the lines of communication open. Some teachers send notebooks home daily sharing details about a child's day at school. This is also a good vehicle for parents to use to communicate with the teacher. Although this approach is most often used for young children, it may be appropriate for older children during transition periods or when medication changes are made. Establish early on with the teacher how you will communicate. Some people prefer written notes; others do better with phone calls.

Building a solid relationship with school personnel naturally results in joint problem-solving. Not only can the teachers help to resolve issues at home, but parents can also offer invaluable input into creative problem-solving for situations at school. Sharing ideas and discussing strategies that have been effective can benefit your child both at home and at school. For example, you may have found a behavior management technique that can also be effective in school. If you are struggling with homework time, your child's teacher may recommend attention-holding techniques that have worked in the classroom. The important thing to remember is that neither you nor the professionals have all the answers. Sharing information can only help you and your child. Teachers are often good sources of information regarding disabilities. They pass along workshop and conference announcements as well as articles and books. The school staff members working with your child can also introduce you to other parents in similar circumstances. Support thus breeds support.

Talking to your child is another effective way to learn how things are at school. Some children will not be able to communicate in a traditional manner, but their behavior often indicates how things are going. If you sense that things are not going well, speak with the teacher or principal.

Visits to the classroom or therapy sessions give parents the opportunity not only to get better acquainted with teachers and therapists, but also to become familiar with the techniques being used. Visits can open discussions about effective strategies at home and at school, and may also alert you to things that are not working at school. Questions or concerns should be discussed promptly with the teacher, therapist, principal, or special education administrator.

Once your child starts in special education, as well as at the beginning of each school year, it is important to know his or her schedule of services. Not only does this aid you in communicating with your child, it is also a vehicle for ensuring that your child is receiving the services outlined in the IEP.

At the start of each school year I get Lara's schedule from her special education teacher and compare it to the IEP. It is then posted on our refrigerator so I can ask Lara specific questions about her day at school.

For many children with disabilities, the beginning of school can be a stressful time. This is particularly true if your child will be meeting new teachers or therapists, or attending different school facilities. It is important to remember that you may call a team meeting at any time. The start of a new school year may be a time when such a meeting is needed.

My daughter will have a new special education teacher for the first time in four years this fall, and I have requested a team meeting for late September. In addition to bringing the team up-to-date on Lara's summer, the meeting will deal with inclusion strategies. I will also relay the things that are important to me in facilitating communication. For example, I like to receive weekly written updates on Lara's progress. The principal, the general and special education teachers, and Lara's father will attend.

In some school districts the special education administrator is such a dominant player that the principal is not included in team meetings. The principal, however, can be a critical player, particularly in matters of inclusion. Time and time again I have heard parents say that the principal was the key to getting their child effectively integrated within the mainstream.

Conferences

Parent/teacher conferences are important to good communication and for assuring that you are up-to-date on your child's progress in school. At the conclusion of a conference you should know how your child is doing on each IEP objective. Some states require school districts to provide a written progress report on each child's IEP. If this is not standard procedure in your school system, ask that such a report be given to you in advance of the meeting.

With some children, or under certain circumstances, a team meeting should be held in place of a conference. This may be necessary in complex cases, during transitions, or if your child is having difficulty in school. It is important to remember that you have the right to convene a team meeting at any time.

A woman whose autistic daughter, Karen,♦ was being integrated with her local middle school convened weekly team meetings. As a result, Karen's move was successful.

Inclusion

Inclusion in general classrooms is becoming more and more a reality for children with disabilities. Children who decades ago would have been institutionalized are now attending neighborhood schools, fully integrated within the mainstream. Although I believe strongly that full inclusion is not right for every child, it has dramatically improved the lives of many children with disabilities and should always be given consideration.

As I have emphasized, the principal can play a key role in making inclusion efforts successful; the efforts of general and special education staff members are also critical. What you may not realize is that a great many ideas and a great deal of support can be generated by other children. Two notable approaches have effectively drawn upon the creativity and willingness to accept children with disabilities so often expressed by children generally. Circle of Friends and MAPS are structured group problem-solving techniques aimed at building peer support networks. When led by experienced facilitators and carried out correctly, they can successfully involve not only classmates but neighborhood children as well. Contact your state PTIC (Parent Training and Information Center) for additional information.

Moving On—Transition Planning

Planning for life after high school can be stressful even in the most ordinary circumstances. Where will your child go to college? How will you/he/she pay for college? Will he/she get accepted? What about the SATs (Standardized Achievement

Tests)? Should he/she seek employment rather than continuing on to college? If you add to these questions or change them entirely, you may have an even more stressful situation. Fortunately, services are available to assist children and parents through this period. Local school districts must follow specific requirements, including the development of the transition section of the IEP.

Regardless of your child's next step after high school or of other services offered under IDEA, transition planning is required by federal law. If your child will continue on to a rehabilitation program, employment, college, or other postsecondary education, early planning will be critical if he or she is to make a smooth transition.

IDEA mandates that transition planning become a priority when a student reaches age 16 (or younger if appropriate). Necessary transition services must be incorporated into the IEP and this planning must be on the agenda at every IEP annual review meeting once the child turns 16. Some states have established a specific agency to assist in transition planning.

The transition section of your child's IEP must include outcomes, instructional goals and objectives, community experiences, employment and postschool adult living, and a description of the interagency responsibilities before the student leaves the school system. These services should be designed to promote a smooth transition from school to postschool endeavors. If your child will be eligible for services under the Rehabilitation Act, plans for these services should be included within the transition process.

College

Professionals are available who offer college placement consulting services. They can inform high school students and their parents about programs available at various colleges and how to go about acquiring services. Many colleges offer special education services ranging from programs designed for learning disabled students to resource room or tutoring services. Some colleges also offer programs for young adults with mental retardation.

When their needs are documented properly, college students with disabilities may be entitled to take untimed tests and to other classroom modifications as needed. All college entrance exams must be offered to eligible students in an untimed fashion. It is best to contact the company administering the test well in advance to learn their documentation requirements. A good high school guidance counselor should be able to help you through this process, but many students and parents find it beneficial instead to work with a professional consultant.

Employment

Should your son or daughter choose to seek employment after high school, the school system must work with him or her through the transition. For example, it may be possible that your child is eligible for some sort of rehabilitation services, including facilitated employment options (see Chapter 5). If your child is not eligible for these services, an agenda item for team meetings beginning at age 16 should be vocational options. Not only should your child's education program be geared toward developing the necessary skills to succeed in a certain vocation, it should also involve helping him or her find a suitable vocation. This can take the form of competency testing, as well as allowing your child to observe or perhaps try out certain vocations before graduation.

Rehabilitation

Children with the most profound disabilities are usually eligible for services even when their eligibility under IDEA ends. As explained in Chapter 5, each state has different guidelines for service eligibility. Regardless of your state's laws, however, IDEA requires joint team meetings with rehabilitation personnel if a student may be eligible for rehabilitation services. Eligibility should be determined before high school graduation or dismissal from other services provided under IDEA.

Rehabilitation services vary dramatically and should be in accordance with the needs of your child. Some young adults may need 24-hour care, others an independent living arrangement, and still others supported employment services. The needs and desires of your child should dictate the services provided. Unfortunately, many states do not adequately fund rehabilitation programs, and families must either help out or see their loved ones go without appropriate services. That is why transition planning is so crucial. You are in a much better position to locate services for your child while he or she is still receiving services under IDEA.

Your Child's Role

Your child's role will be reviewed in detail in Chapter 12. Particularly during transition planning, however, it is essential that your son or daughter have a key role in any decision making. Working toward this goal cannot begin too early. Discussing with your child at age seven or eight what he or she wants to be when grown is the beginning of transition planning. As your child grows older, these conversations can include what it takes to become a lawyer, a carpenter, a grocery bagger, a teacher, or whatever profession your child wants to pursue. Your child should visit places of business to see firsthand what it is like to be an accountant, day care provider, etc..

When formal transition planning begins, your child will be invited to the team meetings. This is required by federal law. Whenever possible, your child should participate in these meetings. To succeed as an adult, he or she must exercise as much independence as feasible. Transition planning is the beginning of adulthood and your child should be encouraged to take responsibility for his or her future.

8 Recreational Activities

We all need breaks from our work, whether that work is taking care of a home or employment outside of the home. Many people believe children learn more out of school than in. Recreational activities afford children the opportunity to tap strengths that may remain hidden in academic settings. Such activities also allow children to experience positive social interactions.

Sporting and club activities can give your child the opportunity to develop language, memory, and learning skills, as well as fine and gross motor skills. These activities also put your child into situations that require greater levels of independence than are needed at school or home. Playmates may push your child through peer pressure or encouragement. Your child may also simply rise to the occasion because he or she is involved in a fun activity.

For some children with disabilities, sports are their primary arena for success.

My brother, now grown and with two children of his own, had difficulty in school due to dyslexia. Cappy excelled at every sport in which he participated. It did not matter to his friends that he was having trouble in school when he was winning races. He was able to draw a large measure of his self-image from his athletic achievements.

Program Types

Recreational activities include sports, clubs, camp, and many other occasions for children to learn and have fun. There are programs specifically for children with disabilities, as well as others that include all children. The right choice for your child will depend on his or her needs and on the particular program.

Sports programs are a part of most school programs, but there are also activities sponsored by local park districts, YMCAs, and other organizations. All programs are potentially open to your child. Many children with spina bifida, for example, participate in gross motor sports such as horseback riding, bowling, and swimming. The Skating Association for the Blind and Handicapped (see Appendix B for contact information) has developed many creative ways for children with disabilities to learn to skate. The Special Olympics has brought joy and success into the lives of thousands of developmentally disabled children and young adults.

Do not overlook your child's school in your search for recreational activities. Section 504 of the Rehabilitation Act of 1973 requires that a child's disability be considered when determining sports eligibility. There are countless success stories, including that of a boy with Down syndrome in Colorado who played on his high school basketball team and scored in a game.

Clubs such as Girl Scouts, Boy Scouts, and Indian Guides may offer other excellent experiences for your child. These groups give children a chance to interact without academic or athletic pressures, focusing primarily on social interactions and community involvement.

If your child is musically inclined, he or she may find a safe harbor in music. Persons with disabilities are often creative and excel in the arts. Fine arts lessons are offered in group as well as private settings, but lessons are not always necessary. Something as simple as encouraging your child to snap photographs can give him or her a chance for creative expression.

Summer camp can provide your child with the opportunity (possibly better than any other experience) to work on social and independence skills. At camp, children practice relationship skills while also learning to care for themselves. There are many different types of camps, including day and overnight, disabilities versus integrated, sports versus general versus fine arts. Camps that offer sports usually offer programs on either gross motor (i.e., water sports) or fine motor activities. Aside from being a positive experience for your child, summer camp can also be a relaxing one for you!

Several support organizations (such as ARC) sponsor and run their own recreational programs. Many YMCAs offer programs for children with disabilities.

My daughter attended a creative movement class for children with disabilities and the experience was as good for me as it was for her. The other mothers and I talked during class, sharing our experiences and discussing how we coped. Lara was relatively young at the time and I was still struggling with how to accept the difference in our lives. Talking with those three other women, all of whom had been at "it" longer, was a great source of emotional support and reinforcement.

Another YMCA in our area offers a Saturday program for children with disabilities and their siblings. It gives siblings a chance to talk about their special brother or sister and express their feelings. The children also participate in creative and athletic activities.

Many places of worship offer specialized religious training.

As Joanne, whose son Jonathan has Down syndrome, looked forward to his Bar Mitzvah, the hassle of hosting an event for 300 people seemed worth every minute.

Finding the Right Programs for Your Child

Finding the right recreational programs for your child can be time consuming. You may want your child to be in a regular program and therefore need to find one with an instructor who is capable of bringing your son or daughter into the activities. A program specifically designed for children with disabilities may be more appropriate for another child. Many support organizations can provide names and descriptions of such programs. The

American Camping Association publishes literature useful in selecting a summer camp.

Involving your child in the search and selection process always helps, no matter what type of program you are looking for. This is especially true as your child grows older, or if he or she has difficulty trying new things. You may have to ease into new programs slowly, giving your child the chance to adjust to the idea.

> *My daughter often resists trying new things. One day when I suggested she start up with swimming lessons again her immediate response was "No!" Instead of pressing my suggestion, as I would have done in the past, I let it drop for a few days after asking Lara to think it over. In a week she agreed, albeit with some grumbling, to try swimming lessons again. After the first lesson she came running up to me and said, "Mommy, you were right, swimming lessons were a good idea. I had fun!"*

Ensuring a Positive Experience for Your Child

As is true for all of us, your child is more likely to have a positive experience in a recreational activity if the activity is something he or she can succeed at and enjoys. Often times, however, you will have to work harder than most parents to ensure a positive experience.

Considering what your objectives are in having your child participate in an activity is a good starting point. If the priority is socialization or improving self-esteem, finding the right level may be easier. If the main objective for your child is participation in the community, Little League with his or her peers may be the best choice. The most important outcome is that your child feels good about the experience and about him or her self.

You may need to talk to the instructors, counselors, or leaders before the first day of activities to let them know your child's strengths and weaknesses and how they may affect participation. Discuss your objectives with the leader and offer to help out if you can.

On camp forms, give all the information you can and share

IEPs, IFSPs, evaluation assessments, and your own documentation. This information will help the camp know your child and assist the counselors who will be working with your child. If the camp seems wary of all the documentation, perhaps it is not the right camp for your child. Most camps, however, are very open to campers with disabilities. For example, the Girl Scout summer camp brochure states, "Girls with special needs are also welcome if they can be mainstreamed into the regular camp program. Girls should be verbal, able to care for their own hygiene, willing, and moderately able to keep up with the daily camp program."

Once your child is in a program, follow up with the leader periodically to see how things are going. Also talk to your child to make sure he or she feels things are okay. If your child is away at sleepover camp and has difficulty reading or writing, use cassette tapes in place of letters. The sound of a parent's voice can be comforting even to a child who is not homesick.

Recreational activities can be rewarding experiences for all children and for the adults involved as well. They can be a chance to demonstrate independence as well as an opportunity to learn compassion and understanding.

When Lara was seven years old, her first Brownie troop leader was leery of her attending an overnight without me. As it turned out, I was unable to chaperone because there were already too many volunteers, so Lara went without me. She was one of the bravest, most independent girls that night. The troop leader realized that her fears were misplaced.

Lara's third Brownie troop leader also found working with a unique child a rewarding experience. She said, "I just spent a little extra time with Lara to get her started on an activity and now she is involved in all the projects. She is my favorite, my pet. I guess that's why we do things like this—to see children have a good experience, to help them grow. Leslie [her daughter] helped Lara in a project that we had done at home the night before. I guess I rubbed off on her, too. It made me feel so good."*

9 Child Day Care

Finding the Right Provider

Chances are that you and your co-parent both work outside the home. Finding good child day care is a considerable responsibility under any condition, but when your child has disabilities, the task of finding a competent and loving child day care provider can be even more challenging. If your child has behavior problems, the provider must be willing and able to manage them effectively. If your child needs special medical attention, the person caring for him or her must be willing to spend the extra time required as well as be able to administer the care responsibly. Your child's unique characteristics must be taken into consideration to ensure a good match with a caregiver.

Many books (such as *The Working Parents' Guide to Child Care*, by Byrna Siegel-Gorelick) and magazine articles about child day care are readily available. Most publications include checklists of questions to ask prospective child day care providers. These publications are excellent places to begin, but you should add your own questions so you can determine whether a prospective caregiver will provide the care your child needs. On the next page are some questions you may want to ask.

You may choose a child day care provider who has never worked with a child with disabilities before. If you are confident that the caregiver is willing and able to learn about your child's

129

Interviewing Child Day Care Providers

In addition to the general questions you might ask of prospective child day care providers, you may also want to obtain answers to some or all of the following questions.

1. Do you know what "special needs" means?
2. Have you cared for a child with disabilities before? What was the child's disability? Where is that child now? May I speak to his or her parents?
3. What do you know about my child's disability? (If the care provider is not familiar with your child's disability, explain it to him or her.) How would you deal with my child?
4. Will you charge me differently?
5. Would you be willing to attend special training if there was no cost to you?
6. Will any of the parents of other children in your care raise questions about your caring for my child?
7. Several books deal with my child's type of disability. Would you be willing to read some that I recommend?

needs, that may satisfy all the necessary criteria. After all, you probably did not have previous experience and look how well you are doing!

Before selecting someone to care for your child, speak with other parents. Discuss the caregiver's strengths and weaknesses. Be open about your child's needs in these conversations and in talking with prospective care providers. Talk over some sample scenarios with child day care providers and parents. For example, if your child has epilepsy, describe what it is like when your child has a seizure. Ask a prospective care provider what he or she would do if such an event were to occur. Find out from other parents how they think the caregiver would respond. Reviewing possible scenarios can allow you to offer suggestions as well as help you to determine whether your child will be well cared for in a particular setting.

Many states as well as employers now offer child day care

referral services. Certain private organizations also provide search and match services. These agencies may be able to help you find an appropriate day care provider or help by reviewing the questions you plan to ask prospective caregivers.

Your Child's Caregiver: Part of the Team

Your child's day care provider is an important member of his or her team. Young children may spend more waking hours with their day care provider than with anyone else. It may be appropriate for your child's caregiver to participate in team meetings. My daughter's preschool/day care teacher attended Lara's first team meeting and was quite helpful in informing the special education team about Lara's strengths and weaknesses.

Educating your child's caregiver about your child's disability and progress is important: it enables the caregiver to provide appropriate care. To help the caregiver better understand your child, share articles and books as well as copies of IEPs, IFSPs, evaluation assessments, and your own plans. If you are concerned about the confidentiality of these records, select those that best describe your child and ask the caregiver to get your permission before showing them to anyone else.

Several agencies provide respite care training to day care providers. You may want to consider this training if your son or daughter has special medical needs or is developmentally disabled. (See Chapter 3 for further information on respite care.)

Your day care provider should be an active participant in your child's behavior management program. Just as it is important to be consistent within your own home, it is also important to maintain consistency between home and day care. If you are using a particular technique, share the book or video with the caregiver and discuss the program with him or her. If your child exhibits different behavior outside your home than inside, the caregiver can be a good resource, helping to identify these variations and potential causes for them. Your child's caregiver is likely to have valuable ideas and opinions. Encourage him or her to share these with you, but be sure you remain in control of how behavior management is carried out.

Children who receive physical, occupational, or speech and language therapy can gain from the involvement of their child day care provider. This is particularly true with younger children. Arrange to have the therapist meet with the caregiver to demonstrate some helpful activities, or if you feel comfortable, demonstrate them yourself. In many cases, it may simply be making the day care provider aware of activities that will benefit your child (such as working with clay for the development of hand muscles), so that your child can be steered in the right direction. Having another knowledgeable member on the team can greatly benefit your child.

All states have regulations regarding child day care, particularly with regard to the administration of medication. Becoming familiar with the regulations before interviewing prospective providers can help you to ask appropriate questions. Inform your child's caregiver in writing and verbally about how and when to administer your child's medication. The caregiver should be aware of potential side effects of any medication.

Lara takes Ritalin and does not eat lunch until 3:30 P.M. when the medication wears off. Communication with Lara's after-school program teachers is necessary to make sure she eats her sandwich before she is allowed to have a snack.

Ideally, child day care will provide a safe haven for your child. Your child should feel comfortable and nurtured. The caregiver you select can reinforce your efforts to improve socialization skills while also encouraging independence. Discuss your goals, objectives, and strategies with your child's day care provider. You and your child's caregiver should become strong partners for the benefit of your child.

10 Family

Your family members may provide you with strong emotional support or they may be a source of frustration and even anger. Many parents of children with disabilities, however, describe their families as the core of their support network and say they would feel lost without them.

What Parents Need and Want

Family members give each other support in times of need. Support can come in the form of financial assistance, child care and advice, or helping one another to maintain emotional stability. Many people look to their parents, siblings, and other family members when they need help. Families of children with disabilities may need more from family members. In this sense, the family itself has special needs.

As the parent of a child with a disability, you may require practical things from your family. Information about your family's medical and educational history may help in your search for a diagnosis. It can also be beneficial as you develop strategies for coping with your child (see Chapter 1 for more information).

Your parents or siblings may be good providers of respite care, giving you and your co-parent the chance to take a break from your children. Many parents feel most comfortable leaving their children with family members. Not only does such care afford you the opportunity to get away, it gives your family a chance to get to know your child better. Spending concentrated time with a grandchild, niece, or nephew with disabilities can educate your family on what life is like in your household. If your child has special medical needs, you may want to consider respite care training for family members caring for your child (discussed in more detail in Chapter 3).

My family lives 900 miles away from Lara and me so we see each other only a few times a year. When we do get together, it is always encouraging to hear my brother and sister comment on Lara's progress. Sometimes I get overwhelmed with day-to-day living and do not notice that Lara is developing. Even family members who live close by can remind you of things your child is now able to do and of problem behaviors that have ceased.

Someone in your family may be the first one to recognize that your child is having difficulty.

> *Jennifer,* ◆ *an elementary school principal and mother of two, is grateful to her sister, who recognized language delays in Jennifer's daughter. Angela* ◆ *received early intervention services and is now in high school, no longer in need of special education.*

Members of your family may be able to offer suggestions on how to work with your child. Perhaps they have some applicable education or have a disability themselves. Or perhaps they also have a child with disabilities and you can learn from each other. If you have a disability, your parents and siblings may be able to help you by remembering how you coped with your disability as a child.

What parents of children with disabilities want most from their families is acceptance of their child. As one mother of a child with ADD lamented:

> *I just want to be able to go to a family gathering and have my son fit in. I mean, that's where you're supposed to be accepted. But they just think he's a bad kid. My heart goes out to my son; I feel so bad for him.*

Your family may not understand that your child needs extra encouragement and that seemingly small accomplishments ought to be acknowledged.

> *When my niece, who is nine months older than my daughter, made her first solo sail on a Sunfish, everyone cheered. When Lara steered the Sunfish by herself with me in the boat, no one said anything. I was so angry and hurt I threw a temper tantrum! My family in general is very accepting of Lara, but the incident made me realize that I should talk with them more about what Lara and I need.*

Acceptance comes more easily in some families than in others and more easily for certain members within a family. It depends on the nature of the disability and on the personalities and personal histories of the family members. Your child may develop a special relationship with one family member, as my friend Marcy's son has done with his aunt. Jacob feels safe in his aunt's home because she has accepted Jacob for who he is.

When Your Family Tries To Help, But in the Wrong Way

My friend Ellen's brother is sure that simply being firm with her daughter Elizabeth will cure her ADD. He loves his sister and his niece and believes he is offering appropriate advice. Your parents may encourage you to believe that your child will grow out of his or her disability, because they do not want you to be hurt. Jacob's grandfather does not yet understand that Jacob will have special needs all his life.

> *Jo Ann's parents disagreed with her decision to put her daughter on Ritalin. Jo Ann finally said to her mother, "Telling Emily to pay attention without Ritalin is like telling a child with epilepsy who's not on medication not to have a seizure!" Once Emily's grandparents were able to see the positive effects of the medication, they did agree that it was the right thing to do.*

Just as you have educated yourself about your child's disabilities, so should you educate your family. Hiding or covering up the truth serves only to confuse a stressful situation. If family members are having difficulty accepting your child, share information with them. Select articles or books that connect with their concerns or misunderstandings. Bring them to workshops with you or have them watch an appropriate movie or video. As you know firsthand, acceptance can be painful and it may take a long time. Having a clearer understanding of your child's disability can help.

If you are really brave, include your extended family members in planning sessions for your child. Many school systems use a group problem-solving technique called Circle of Friends (explained in more detail in Chapter 6). A similar approach may be effective for your family. Circle of Friends facilitates the people in your child's life working together to include him or her in a regular classroom. Modified to fit your situation, it may be an effective way to fully include your child in the whole family.

Some members of your family may refuse to learn about your child's disability or they may disagree with how you are managing your child's care or education. It is frustrating when someone does not want to educate themselves about your situation. If this lack of knowledge adversely affects your child, you may want to consider enlisting the help of more supportive family members. Ask someone else in your family to carry the ball in your behalf. It is important to start small, with easy-to-understand literature or videos. If the situation becomes severe, a mental health professional may be able to help you to work out a strategy for your particular predicament.

In any event, as a parent, you are the one responsible for your child's care. Family members often offer unwanted advice, particularly to new parents. When advice turns to aggressive disagreement, you should take action. Explain to the members of your family who disagree with your approaches that, while you appreciate their concern and even at times their advice, you have selected your way for certain reasons. If the other person cannot accept how you are managing your child, perhaps interactions between you, your child, and that family member will have to be limited. This may seem harsh, but your child's well-being has priority.

When a Family Member Ignores the Situation or the Child

Families and friends often compare cousins to one another. This can be a painful experience for you when your child has a disability. You may tend to be overly sensitive and may assume a comparison is being made even when one is not intended.

My best high school friend commented on what bright children my sister had and wasn't it amazing how exceptional they all were. Her words stung and still do. But Amy was not comparing Lara to her cousins, she was praising my sister and her family. Nonetheless, I often react first as Lara's mother.

When there are achieving children, or especially, overachieving children, in an extended family, children with disabilities may be ignored. A grandfather may choose to go fishing with his mature and conversational granddaughter and leave the one with a language disorder behind.

In some ways this reaction may be easier to tolerate than the grandmother who does not believe in your behavior management approach. It is easier to protect a child from being ignored by a family member than from a family member who is undermining the parent's authority. It is also easier to ignore the ignoring or at least not to deal with it. If the situation should become unbearable, however, you should draw the erring family member in slowly. It is probably not wise to dump a 300-page book on your sister's lap and say, "I'm tired of you not accepting the reality that Jamie is autistic and that it's not my fault. Read this book!" Enlisting the assistance of a family member who is more understanding may help—your brother may be less emotional and therefore better able to communicate with your mother.

It has been easy for me to avoid confronting my father with how it hurts me and Lara when he ignores his granddaughter. Although we have always done many things together, my father and I have had few heart-to-heart conversations and we see each other only a couple of times a year. This past Christmas, which I spent in my home town while Lara was with her father, I decided to try to do something about it.

> *My father is creative and works with wood as a hobby. He crafted a beautiful piece of furniture for my niece's doll and an innovative stove for my nephew. He gave Lara a hat and mittens. Although I did not confront him (someday perhaps I will), I did write him a letter explaining that Lara, like many people with learning disabilities, was having difficulty comprehending time and could he build something that would put a year, months, weeks, and days in concrete terms. I spoke with him the other day and he has a design in mind.*

This is the first step toward what I hope will bring about an acceptance of my daughter by my father. I plan to write him again, explaining Lara and her needs. And possibly I will recommend some reading material, specifically about Lara and others with her disabilities. I do not expect my father to fully understand Lara, I just want the two of them to share some good times together.

Your Other Children

Life with a sibling who has disabilities has its ups and downs. Some siblings feel cheated of the sibling they had wished for and cheated out of time with their parents. Despite the difficulties, however, most siblings of people with disabilities have many positive experiences. According to T.H. Powell and P.A. Ogle, authors of *Brothers and Sisters: A Special Part of Exceptional Families,* siblings often achieve high levels of empathy and altruism, accept differences more than most, have a heightened sense of maturity and responsibility, and are proud of their siblings' accomplishments. Not surprisingly, many brothers and sisters of people with disabilities enter professions that help the disabled population.

Sibling Feelings

Siblings of children with disabilities respond to their circumstances on a continuum. At one end of the continuum is the child who is exceedingly "good"—well-behaved and overachieving. At the opposite end of the continuum is the sibling who reacts outwardly with aggression, frustration, and anger. Although the behavior of the child at the "good" end of the continuum may be a relief to some parents, it should be a warning signal.

Dianne,♦ mother of a five-year-old son with ADD, worries that her three-year-old daughter is trying to be a "perfect" child. Rightly so, Dianne is concerned that Jenny♦ is taking on the responsibility of her parents' happiness.

The mother of two young adults with ADD and obsessive-compulsive disorder related how her younger, better be-haved, and less needy son fell apart when her older son left home for college.

Confusion tends to arise in households prior to a diagnosis. In some cases, anxiety and even fear may be felt during this period. These emotions can be felt by the entire family, including the child with disabilities and the brothers and sisters. In households where these feelings go unspoken and undiscussed, siblings' imaginations can become quite active. They may wonder if they caused the disability or they may fear that they will one day catch it.

Brothers and sisters may also worry about the future. If the prognosis for a sibling is not discussed, a brother or sister may think the result will be death. The longer siblings are kept in the dark about the challenges facing a brother or sister with disabilities, the greater the likelihood of unrealistic expectations and misunderstandings. No matter what the age of your other children, they need to be told, in words they can understand, about their brother or sister. Many children's books are available that explain different disabilities (see Appendix C.). Read these to your children and discuss how the disability affects your special child and the rest of your family. Even if you think your child without disabilities is too young and cannot understand, you may be surprised at how much he or she already comprehends about the disability.

Caring for your child with disabilities may take extra time and energy. Some of this time and energy will come at the expense of your other children. This may seem unfair to them and to the rest of your family. But as Richard Lavoie relates in his *Fat City* video, fairness is giving a child what he or she needs. Since children need different things, being fair does not always result in each child receiving the same thing. If siblings have trouble accepting this definition of fairness, ask them if it would be fair to take a student's glasses away because the rest of the children in the class do not have glasses. This definition of fairness can also be helpful in dealing with the reaction to different rules you may have for your children.

Despite the unequal amounts of energy that go toward your children, each of your children need special time with you and your co-parent. Make a point to set aside a certain part of each day to read alone with them or to have a private conversation. Or share special time each week, a time when your other children have you all to themselves. This time can be used to talk about what it is like to have a brother or sister with disabilities. More importantly, it can be a time to talk about your other children's friends and how they are doing in school, sports, or other activities. This designated time with you or your co-parent can help dispel the natural anger directed at you, your co-parent, and the sibling with disabilities because of the extra attention your child with a disability requires.

Siblings may feel anger when they are told to be understanding and accepting of their brother or sister with disabilities. They may also resent having to go along on doctors' appointments or therapy sessions. One mother, whose daughter with disabilities attends weekly speech therapy sessions and requires frequent trips to the doctor, arranges for her other daughter to play with friends during these appointments whenever possible. Feelings of anger and animosity can lead to guilt. Siblings may also feel guilty because they are "normal" and wish their brother or sister could be "normal" as well.

Suppressed feelings of frustration, anger, and guilt can lead to sadness and sometimes depression. It is important for the development of siblings that they be allowed to express their feelings in constructive ways. Programs for siblings are offered at some YMCAs, hospitals, and clinics, and can give children an opportunity to talk about what life is like with a sibling with disabilities. In some circumstances, individual or family counseling may be necessary to work through these feelings.

The acceptance of a sibling with disabilities through understanding of the disability can lead to the acceptance of your child by others.

> *Jimmy,*♦ *whose older brother has severe ADD, says that it is "no big deal" to have his friends over because they understand his brother; Jimmy has told them about his brother's disability.*

> *Michael,*♦ *whose brother has Tourette's syndrome and obsessive-compulsive disorder, finds it difficult at times to have friends over but in general feels comfortable explaining his brother's difficulties to others. Michael's parents have been open about his brother's disabilities since Michael was very young.*

All of these feelings are natural for the siblings of a child with disabilities. It is also normal for siblings to act out in order to attract attention. Some children may even create their own "disability" as a means of getting attention. Discussing the challenges your family faces can help with these feelings. Siblings will most likely be relieved to hear that you are disappointed too; that you feel cheated out of a "normal" family. Siblings also should know that it is okay for them to get angry with their brother or sister who has a disability. Through open and honest communication, all of your children can accept the differences in your lives.

Making Siblings Part of the Team

The first step to making siblings contributing members of your child's team is communication. Educating your children on the nature of their sibling's disability is crucial if your family is to work as a team. Information puts fears into perspective and opens the gates to productive discussions in the future.

There is a fine line between too much and too little responsibility for children who have a brother or sister with disabilities. Although parents should resist the temptation to allow their other children, particularly older girls, to become another parent to the child with a disability, all siblings do have a certain level of responsibility to one another, regardless of any special needs. As one mother at a conference I attended said:

> *Kids have more energy than we do. They often have creative solutions to their siblings' problems.*

Engage siblings in conversations about how to manage some aspects of your child with disabilities. Ask them to describe their brother or sister as an adult. Or ask them what behavior bothers them the most and how they think it should be managed. This can be a useful approach when siblings are frustrated because they think you are not caring appropriately for their brother or sister. You can do this informally as well as including all your children in your formal planning for their sibling.

To encourage empathy on the part of siblings, some authors recommend having siblings of children with disabilities attend school for a day with their brother or sister. Experiencing classroom activities and therapy sessions removes some of the mystery and promotes a better understanding of what life is like for a sibling with a disability. This approach can be helpful for children with older or younger siblings with disabilities.

Siblings of children with disabilities often feel mature and find it rewarding when they help their brother or sister, or when they help you by providing respite care. Siblings can also model appropriate behavior, as well as teach their brother or sister new skills. A brother and sister felt triumphant when they taught their physically disabled sister to climb the stairs.

Social interactions outside the family may sometimes be limited for a child with disabilities. This places more significance on the relationship between siblings. Although your child's siblings may be his or her friends as well, it is important that you encourage friendships outside the family for all your children.

Your family will have a great impact on the life of your child with disabilities, and your child's siblings may have a greater impact than you expect. Not only will your children likely outlive you and perhaps one day provide care for your child with a disability in his or her adulthood, but your children in many ways define your family. They can nurture and support each other throughout their lives. Even at a young age, siblings can offer comfort and support.

> *A three-year-old girl whose adolescent sister was temporarily leaving home for a psychiatric hospital said as she stroked her sister's cheek, "I'll take care of your toys while you're gone."*

The adjustment by your other children to the impact your child with disabilities has on your family can affect the development of self-esteem in all of your children.* Sibling issues are increasingly on the agendas of conferences and the topics of workshops. Some support organizations and newsletters are dedicated to siblings of children with disabilities (see Appendixes B and C). Powell and Ogle, in *Brothers and Sisters: A Special Part of Exceptional Families*, offer several useful strategies for parents.

Families can look upon a disability as a burden or, as eloquently stated by a woman whose sibling had disabilities:

> *For all families: Use your differences and your gifts to imagine the fullest life each family member can live. There is a difference between being "disabled" and "having a disability." If I am "disabled," that defines who I am. If I "have a disability," I have certain choices as to how this physical and psychological reality limits what I do and how I live. If other people recognize and respect that disability, we can work together to create ways to stretch those limits."* * *

---

* Horne, Schmieg, Place, Smith, Prickett, and Valdivieso, "Children with Disabilities: Understanding Sibling Issues," *NICHY News Digest* 11 (1988).
** "I Never Figured You Were Disabled — A Sister's Experience," *Children with Disabilities: Understanding Sibling Issues,* NICHY News Digest 11 (1988).

11 Friends

For many people, friendships are the most important relationships in their lives. We play with friends, we help our friends, and in return, we receive support from our friends. For children, friendships, in many ways, define who they are.

Your Friends

Often, different friends fulfill different needs for you. Some friends are your buddies—people with whom you do fun things but the relationship is not intimate. Some friends are former schoolmates. With some, you may have a professional friendship—someone from work with whom you lunch on occasion. There are also friendly neighbors and friendly acquaintances. When your child has disabilities, you may draw a good deal of support from the friendly acquaintances you meet because of your child's disability.

In the years since Lara entered special education I have come to know many other parents (mostly mothers) of children with disabilities. Most of these relationships have grown out of my association with my local special education parent advisory council, but some have resulted from talking with other parents during our children's swimming lessons or other activities.

Although I do not have a close relationship with any of these women, they have been a tremendous source of support. Being able to talk openly about Lara, her disabilities, and the impact of Lara's special needs on me is liberating. In most cases, they and I have little else in common, yet they are high on my list of support providers. Even within this group of friends, each provides a different type of support and comfort. I call upon some for advocacy support, some for respite support, and others for emotional support. I also take satisfaction in providing these kinds of support in return.

Attending local parent support group meetings offers an excellent opportunity to meet other parents who are facing similar challenges (see Chapter 3). Such relationships may take time to develop. I found volunteering for the board of my local special education parent advisory council to be the best way for me to establish and maintain these important relationships. You may also want to ask your child's special education teacher or the special education administrator for names of other parents who may be of help. Many parents are willing to offer assistance to other parents regarding children with disabilities.

Although other parents of children with disabilities can offer exceptional support in different ways, you may find that you do not form intimate relationships with them. Having only one thing in common naturally puts a boundary around the potential for the growth of the friendship. Your intimate relationships may be limited to your spouse and close family members. This may be your personal style and have nothing to do with your being the parent of a child with disabilities. Or you may find that having a child with a disability makes it more difficult to develop close relationships with others. As one mother put it:

My friends don't really offer support. I'm so sick of hearing that I'm a saint, 'cause I'm not.

My sister Jean is my closest friend. Unlike my other friends, I can discuss any aspect of mothering Lara with Jean. A friend like this can offer an objective opinion at times when perhaps a spouse or family member cannot. Such friends may not understand your child's disability, or the special education process, but they understand you. This understanding allows a close friend to help you sort through feelings of inadequacy and helplessness. When I am having what I call a "bad mother day," Jean reminds me of my strong points and says that it is probably healthy for Lara to see me on off days. She encourages me to think of "good mother days" and reminds me that I am human, too. Jean also listens to my hopes and dreams for Lara, adding a dose of reality to keep my expectations in line.

It is seldom easy to hear reality from a close friend or any one else. Your reaction may be quite negative or protective (either of your child or yourself) when someone close to you offers advice.

For months I adamantly disagreed with a former boyfriend that I was inconsistent in my dinner table rules for Lara; I allowed my emotions to get in the way of reason. Over time, though, I played through dinnertime scenarios in my head and, begrudgingly, realized that he was right.

It is difficult for most people to listen to criticism and advice. It seems particularly difficult for parents of children with disabilities. Perhaps it is because we may hear so many negative things about our children. Perhaps it is because we feel burdened with our responsibilities; we feel we are working so hard to do a good job that we wonder how anyone could fail to appreciate it.

I am extremely fortunate to have a friend with whom I can share my nightmares and my hopes—someone who lifts me when I am down, and who shares my enthusiasm when I am up. Jean has always supported me as Lara's mother.

Cultivating an intimate relationship is unique to the members of that relationship, as well as to the circumstances that bring and keep them together. A universal component of intimacy, though, is communication and trust. You must feel able to trust the other person with your feelings and be willing to listen to his or her ideas and opinions. The communication must include a sharing of your child's needs. As long as you hide any aspect of your child's disability, trust and openness are not possible.

It is unlikely that you are very close with more than a few persons. Most of your friendships have likely grown out of common interests and experiences and are maintained at that level. Friendships come and go; as you reach milestones in your life, some people will leave your life and other people enter it. The onset of parenthood often brings new persons into your life. It may also change existing friendships. Friends who already have children of their own may become close friends and invaluable sources of ideas and advice. Friends without children can offer much-needed breaks from talk about children. When you learned the diagnosis for your child, you also passed a major milestone. As I have said throughout this book, many new people enter your life at this point. Some of those people will become your friends.

You may have friends with whom you do not discuss your child. Although some parents feel the need to disclose their child's disabilities to all their friends, it may be healthy to have some friendships with whom IEPs and physical therapy are *not* topics of conversation. You may have times in your life when you need to not be the parent of a child with disabilities, but want the opportunity to just be you.

Some parents of children with disabilities find it difficult to sustain relationships with friends who do not understand life with such a child.

> *One mother of a child with severe ADD and Turner's syndrome finds it frustrating because her friends do not know how lucky they are to have a "normal" family. She has trouble sympathizing with her friends' problems because they seem simple compared to hers.*

> *Sharon,♦ the parent of a "normal" child, is unhappy about her friend who has a language-delayed preschooler. Sharon suggested that her friend's daughter be tested, thinking the little girl might be eligible for early intervention services. Sharon's friend resisted, insisting there was nothing wrong with her child. Although her friend did not pursue early intervention services, Sharon continued to offer help.*

Sharon found she could reassure her friend about behaviors that are normal for a child her daughter's age, as well as point out areas of concern.

Having a friend to count on can offer a valuable sense of security. A friend may not fully understand what you are going through, but merely having someone who will listen and who will offer you a shoulder to cry on can help you get through times of need.

Your Child's Friends

Judith Snow, an adult with disabilities, believes "The only disability is having no relationships." Fostering healthy friendships between your child and his or her peers can be essential to your child's happiness. Regardless of the severity of your child's disability, he or she can and should have friends. Friends are an important part of your child's support network.

In addition to the traditional advantages of friendship, children with disabilities can gain much more from their friends. For children with severe disabilities who are included within general education classrooms, friends and classmates often serve as advocates.

Classmates of William,♦ a nonverbal boy with cerebral palsy, stand up for their friend. They make certain he participates in all class activities, including lying on the ground to look up at the leaves in a tree, swimming, and hiking in the mountains. As Betsy,♦ William's mother, says, "Friendships with William don't have different rules."

My daughter and her best friend learn from each other. Marianne, Jessica's mother, commented on how Lara helped Jess get in touch with her feelings—that was something Jessica was having trouble with and it is something Lara is good at. And Lara told her speech and language pathologist, "Jessica has taught me how to be a good friend."

By nature, young children are accepting of others. Studies indicate that people are more accepting of disabilities when they are exposed to them at a young age. The children in your community can learn a great deal from interacting with your child with disabilities. Children will often ask direct questions. Answering in an informative way will help your child be accepted by his or her peers.

Tell the people in your neighborhood and community what your child's disability is. There are many books for children that explain various disabilities (see Appendix C). Visit your child's school and read these books to your child's class. Encourage the children to ask questions and talk about disabilities.

> *After I read* What Do You Mean I Have A Learning Disability? *to my daughter's second grade class, Lara's friend Jessica commented, "That was a good book you read, Lizanne. It helped me understand things better."*

If your child is relatively young, it is important to be forthright with the parents of his or her friends. Explaining your child's disability to these parents will help them better understand your child. In many cases you need not go into much detail (merely tell them your child has a learning disability, for example). Use language and terms they are able to understand. For example, if your child has an auditory lag (a type of learning disability), explain that your child has an auditory processing problem that results in him or her taking longer to grasp what is said. Analogies for describing children with ADD are also quite helpful. For example, having ADD is like listening to a radio with static or like having someone with a remote control constantly changing TV channels. Unexplained disabilities, particularly invisible ones such as ADD or learning disabilities, can cause confusion, with inappropriate conclusions being drawn. Although it may be difficult at first to discuss these topics, it does get easier. Through the years I have never been distressed by anyone's reaction. I have found that those with whom I have been the most open have become the most accepting of my daughter.

12 Your Special Child: A Member of the Team

I have tried throughout this book to talk with you as one parent to another, but this book is really written for our children. It is the present as well as the future that causes us concern and leads us to search for answers, but at some point, at some level, our children with disabilities must begin to take responsibility for themselves. The earlier you begin to instill independence in your child, the more likely your child will lead a happy and fulfilled life.

Choices and Goals

Beginning with simple things, such as giving your child choices, makes the transition to some level of independence easier for both of you. You may allow your child to decide which outfit to wear, or whether your family will have peas or corn with dinner.

As your child becomes able, involve him or her in setting objectives. Periodically, Lara and I decide what three objectives she will work on and agree on how we will keep track of her progress. We vary the ways we follow her progression, with one exception—they must always be visual. For example, sometimes we mark her calendar or use stickers, and sometimes we use a goal chart. Variety helps keep your child and you interested.

Offering your child the opportunity to select three objec-

151

tives from a list of five or six sometimes helps to steer the objectives in the right direction. Some parents find a point system effective for older children, with long-term goals as well as short-term objectives. For example, a child may earn one point each day for each objective met. At the end of one month the child earns a big reward if he or she has earned a certain number of points.

The overall intent of a goal program is to have your child take responsibility for his or her actions and behavior. Other objectives may include improving behavior and/or skills in certain areas. Underlying all of these programs is the ultimate goal of having your child improve his or her self-image. A person who has self-confidence and a positive sense of self-worth can accomplish almost anything!

Once you have determined whether you want to concentrate on behavior or skills, the next step is to select the behaviors you want to encourage or eliminate, or the skills you want to improve. For example, your child may be a whiner and you would like this behavior to diminish. Or you may want your child to improve his or her reading ability.

Formulating objectives to help your child reach the goals is the next task. Objectives are more specific than goals and, when achieved, result in progress toward a goal. There are six important things to remember when developing goals and objectives.

1. The goals should be measurable and not subjective.
2. The objective should be attainable, while at the same time pushing your child to progress.
3. The time horizon should be short.
4. The objective should be a positive statement (I will...).
5. The reward should be immediate and commensurate with the accomplishment.
6. The program should be carried out consistently.

For any goal-setting program to be effective, whether for a child with disabilities, a "typical" child, or an adult, the goals must be objective. This means they must be measurable and specific. "Joe will read for 20 minutes each night" is an example of an objective goal, while "Joe will read more" is an example of a subjective goal.

A child should be encouraged to succeed. The likelihood of a goals program succeeding is greatly increased when the objectives you set are attainable. Start with objectives you are confident your child can achieve, then steadily increase the stretch until the goal is achieved. Objectives should be achievable over a short period of time; it may take years to achieve a goal.

A good objective is stated in a positive fashion. In other words, start the objective with "I will" versus "I will not." "I will keep my bed dry" is much more positive than "I will not wet the bed." Keep the objective focused on what you want your child to do, rather than on what you do not want done.

The acknowledgment that your child is making progress toward objectives and goals should be frequent and tied to a specific event. A child whose objective is to read a book for 20 minutes a day and who will be rewarded with a sticker, should have the sticker placed on his or her chart or calendar as soon as the reading time is complete.

Once you begin a goal program, you must follow through with it. If you drop it part way through, your child is getting a mixed message—does my parent want me to learn to skip or not?

Depending on your child's developmental age, formulating a goals program may be the point at which he or she becomes involved in the decision-making. You may say to him, "Mike, we need to work together to make you a better reader. Do you have any ideas?" Some possible objectives are:

- I will read a book five days a week.
- I will read for 20 minutes each day.
- I will read one book a week.

If one of the goals for your child is to refrain from physically harming others, the following are possible objectives:

- I will play with others for an hour each day without hurting anyone.
- I will have no more than three time-outs for hurting others each day.
- I will have no fights in school.

With a goals program, you can help your child achieve some short-term as well as long-term goals. Using a visual reminder of how your child is doing also serves to remind your child and you just how well he or she is progressing.

Educating Your Child

For children with disabilities to advocate for themselves, they must understand their strengths and weaknesses. They must also understand how they achieve success. By performing goal-setting programs and following through, your child will learn to best accomplish tasks.

Beyond understanding how to reach objectives and eventually goals, your child must also learn as much as possible about his or her particular disabilities. For some, this may mean knowing the name of the disability or personal abilities and limitations; others may know not only the name but also understand technically how the disability has affected them and can describe what classroom modifications are necessary for success. Children with disabilities should, if possible, also learn about the laws that ensure their rights and services.

More and more books are becoming available for children that describe various disabilities. Some, like *What Do You Mean I Have A Learning Disability?*, are geared toward educating the child with the disability, as well as other readers. Others, such as *Loving Ben*, by Elizabeth Laird, deal with the concerns of friends, neighbors, and relatives, although they are also helpful to the child with disabilities.

At times you may think you are alone in your efforts to ensure your child's happiness. Remember that there is always at least one other person who wants to see happiness just as much if not more than you do—your child. Making your child with a disability a partner in his or her own behalf not only lightens your burden in the short-term, but also encourages your child's independence, a key component to a positive self-image and happiness.

Common Challenges

Although the spectrum of disabilities is wide, many of the same issues and challenges affect children with disabilities. These challenges have a common continuum from normal to severe. Some children with a more complex disability such as cerebral palsy may have normal-to-moderate elements in many areas; others with a learning disability may have normal-to-severe elements in fewer areas. The important thing to remember is that you are not alone. You can learn from parents whose children have entirely different disabilities, as well as from parents of "typical" children.

According to a 1987 University of Kansas study, adults with learning disabilities identified the following abilities as being the most critical to their success: self-confidence, effective communication, decision-making, making friends, and getting along with family and in close relationships. These areas are important to most adults with or without disabilities. And within the population of persons with disabilities (regardless of type), success in these areas can greatly improve their lives.

One challenge common to children with disabilities is difficulty with cause-and-effect relationships; this is especially true for children who are blind, learning disabled, mentally retarded, or who have low or below-average intelligence. Also, children with cognitive disabilities have more difficulty learning to compensate for them, requiring more time and patience to master skills.

The remainder of this chapter concentrates on three problem areas common to children with many different disabilities and abilities: behavior, socialization, and organization and integration.

Behavior Problems

When a boy with cerebral palsy said to a boy with an "invisible" disability, "I was born to be in a chair," the latter said, "I was born to be bad."

Behavior problems affect not only children but everyone around them. Worst of all, however, as evidenced by the quote above, is the negative self-image that behavior problems can cause in a child. According to many behavior specialists and parents, however, behavioral problems can be unlearned.

Behavior management is used in everyday life in many settings. Managers use behavior management techniques all the time to encourage staff members to work toward common goals. Parents of all children face behaviors they wish to encourage as well as discourage.

Behavior management is part of a child's school program if the team considers it necessary and documents it in the IEP. For children with autism or ADD, behavior modification may be the core of a program; a child with learning disabilities or mental retardation, on the other hand, may have just one goal dealing with behavior. If your child is receiving behavior management at school, it is important that home and school manage behavior consistently. Discussing effective techniques with your child's teacher can help both you and the teacher.

Feelings of low self-esteem and continual failure can escalate into emotional difficulties for your child. It is important to watch for warning signs, including depression, hostile behavior, withdrawal, or bizarre behavior. Consult a mental health professional at the earliest sign of emotional disturbance.

Many books, workshops, and videos discuss behavior management techniques. *The Difficult Child*, by Dr. Stanley Turecki, contains many solid recommendations for use with preschool children, and *1-2-3: Magic!*, a video by Dr. Thomas Phelan, is an excellent resource for managing behavior in children age three through 14, as is his book, *Surviving Your Adolescence*, about behavior in older children.

Behavior management clinics and specialists can be found within many hospitals. Clinics typically run programs for children as well as parents and often include home visits and evening workshops.

As your child grows, he or she may wear out approaches that have been useful earlier. When this happens, vary the program to meet his or her changing needs. This may entail only slightly altering your existing techniques , switching to a drastically different approach, or trying something unconventional.

> *In an effort to teach my daughter to follow directions, we practiced good behavior by directing Lara to eat a cookie!*

I also try to anticipate difficult situations (like grocery shopping) and discuss them with Lara beforehand.

Most importantly, you must focus consistently on the positive and reward your child for doing the right thing.

Socialization

For some children with disabilities, social skills are a strength. For many, however, interacting with others is difficult. Problems with socialization may be the core of a child's disability or they may be a side effect of immature language skills.

Being accepted by our peers and family members is important to all of us, regardless of ability or disability. Our ability to share experiences and feelings successfully with others is often at the center of our self-esteem. Helping your child build strong social skills will also help him or her to become a stronger self-advocate, as many of the same skills apply.

Many schools and hospitals provide socialization counseling. These programs often use group problem-solving and situation-modeling techniques to help children learn appropriate social behaviors. While structured group settings help to build a foundation, parents can do many things on their own. Simply playing games with your child teaches him or her how to take turns, an important social skill. Exposing your son or daughter to real-life social interactions whenever possible is also healthy. Let your child see you having a conversation with a friend, or talking on the phone. Of course your child should be given the opportunity to practice social skills with friends in formal and informal settings.

If you are concerned about placing your child in a difficult situation, role model the event beforehand, if possible.

> *Lara wanted to have a slumber party to celebrate her birthday. To keep things manageable, I limited the num-*

ber of guests to five and Lara was unfortunately unable to invite all of her friends. I knew one girl would be very upset to find she was not invited and I was not sure Lara would handle it appropriately. By acting out the situation, we were able to discuss how her friend would feel and what Lara should say. As a result, Lara took the initiative and told her friend the next morning. Although both were upset, they discussed it openly and there were no tears.

Using the telephone is often difficult for children with disabilities. This is particularly true for the hearing or language impaired. Again, practicing using the phone can help. Have your child pretend to call someone and you play the other person. Before your child picks up the real phone to place or answer a call, run through a quick drill of how to initiate or answer a call. Good phone skills become increasingly important as children enter adolescence, so practicing when he or she is younger can help your child build solid friendships.

Organization and Integration

People with disabilities often have problems with organization. This can have to do with organizing themselves or organizing information (often referred to as integration). Although they are in many ways different matters, techniques that help in one area can help your child become better organized in another, leading to greater independence.

People often associate organization with neatness. People who can organize themselves by having the right things in the right place may well have an advantage over those who must rummage through their desk to find something. Many people who are outwardly disorganized, however, are internally organized. They can integrate information effortlessly and determine cause and effect relationships spontaneously.

Some people, though, who appear to be very organized, have problems with integration. My daughter's room, for example, is almost always very neat, but at the age of ten she still has great difficulty with the concept of time. Her internal monitors do not provide her with a correct sense of time. People who have problems with sequencing also tend to have problems with organization. They know they have lots of things to do, but do not know which to do next.

Providing your child with external organization aids can help him or her to organize, as well as help compensate for immature integration. Lists are possibly the single most effective technique for this. The process of making a list compels one to sort out one's thoughts before acting. Thus, for the person with integration problems, the act of formulating a list becomes a good problem-solving exercise. The actual creation of the list, whether written or drawn, puts things in black and white. Once made, the list also serves as a wonderful source of positive reinforcement. I know I feel good when I can check things off my list. Making things visual helps children with disabilities see their progress while also reinforcing the concept of order.

A similar technique can help with school assignments. Forming an outline will help your child to gather and organize his or her thoughts before trying to write a paper or do a science project. Using lists reinforces the importance of planning ahead—it reminds impulsive children to stop before they act.

An important point to remember when working with your child on new tasks is to teach him or her how to approach a task versus how to do the task itself. In other words, help your child break down a task by asking him or her to list the subtasks. For example, getting ready for bed has several subtasks. At bedtime, ask your child to name the things to do to get ready for bed. This is simply another list, which you may or may not need to have in visual format. For a child with severe sequencing or memory problems, making a card with pictures of the different steps to be done in getting ready for bed will increase the level of independence while reinforcing good organization. Laminating the card will help it last longer by protecting it from water and toothpaste.

Posting daily and weekly schedules can also build a stronger sense of time and a good foundation for organizational skills. Including your son or daughter in discussions about daily and long-term plans can reinforce these important skills.

Homework is a frequent source of frustration for parents and children. Poor organizational skills aggravate the situation, and an assignment notebook is essential to success. Many options are available, including some for personal computers. For children with poor handwriting, using a tape recorder to document homework assignments can be a lifesaver.

You may ask yourself, "How can I get my child organized when I'm totally disorganized myself?!" Clinics and schools often offer programs to improve organization skills, with many focusing on good study habits. A good psychologist or tutor can also work with your child on improving organizational skills.

13 Pulling It All Together

Being the parent of a child with a disability is not easy, nor is it easy to be a person with a disability. Parents and children must overcome unique obstacles to achieve success and must often redefine success. We have a definition, penned by an unknown writer, posted on our refrigerator:

> *To laugh often and much; to earn the respect of intelligent people and affection of children; to earn the appreciation of honest critics and endure the betrayal of false friends; to appreciate beauty, to find the best in others; to leave the world a bit better, whether by a healthy child, a garden patch, or a redeemed social condition; to know even one life has breathed easier because you have lived. This is to have succeeded.*

As parents of special children, we know our children best. We look at all aspects of our children to fully understand them so we may help them leverage their strengths to overcome their weaknesses. We tend to focus more on real world skills, knowing that few adults are asked to conjugate verbs or recite the capitals of the states. We become creative problem-solvers because we know our children often learn differently. Perhaps an old proverb says it best:

If you tell me, I forget.
If you show me, I see.
If you involve me, I understand.

I like to tag a fourth line onto this proverb: "If you believe in me, I succeed." And success breeds success, which leads to a positive self-image, confidence, and a willingness to try. When Lara begins to give up on something, I sing the first line of her "theme" song by Jimmy Cliff: "You can get it if you really want, but you must try, try, and try, you'll succeed at last."

Tips and Reminders

I hope that you have found the ideas and suggestions in this book of use to you and your child. As you continue to work for and with your child, keep in mind the following tips:

1. You know your child better than anyone else.
2. "Immature" and "developmentally delayed" are red-flag words.
3. Be realistic about your child, the school system, doctors, and yourself.
4. Work with the system, yet stand up for what you know to be right.
5. Don't underestimate your child or yourself.
6. Think long term.
7. Take one day at a time.
8. Chances are, people want what is best for your child.
9. Your child did not ask to have a disability.

Most of all, remember: You are not alone!

Final Thoughts

Life as Lara's mother is a challenge. A month or so before she turned ten I had almost given up hope that Lara would ever learn how to skip. She and I worked on it, her physical therapist and she worked on it, and her dad and she worked on it. For years, I thought this was just going to be one of those things she was not going to be able to do.

A few weeks later Lara and I were at a restaurant for dinner and Lara went to the ladies' room. As I looked up from my menu I saw my daughter bound out of the restroom and skip to the table in beautiful symmetry. My heart filled with pride. Lara was grinning from ear to ear and exclaiming how she had been practicing at recess and every chance she got, and she did it!

Lara surprises me with her insight from time to time. When I was telling her that her great-grandmother had died, she began talking about heaven. She said, "Mom, a lot of people think God is in heaven. But I know he's right here in my heart."

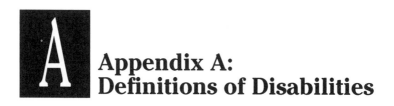

Appendix A:
Definitions of Disabilities

Definitions help describe your child (the nature of the disability) for you and for others. The following definitions, except where noted otherwise, are from IDEA.

Attention Deficit Disorder (ADD)

Characteristics of ADD (from CH.A.D.D. ADD Fact Sheet):

1. Often fidgets with hands or feet or squirms in seat (in adolescence may be limited to subjective feelings of restlessness).
2. Has difficulty remaining seated when required to do so.
3. Is easily distracted by extraneous stimuli.
4. Has difficulty awaiting turn in games or group situations.
5. Often blurts out answers to questions before they have been completed.
6. Has difficulty following through on instructions from others (not due to oppositional behavior or failure of comprehension).
7. Has difficulty sustaining attention in tasks or play activities.
8. Often shifts from one uncompleted activity to another.
9. Has difficulty playing quietly.
10. Often talks excessively.
11. Often interrupts or intrudes on others, e.g., butts into other children's games.
12. Often does not seem to listen to what is being said to him or her.

13. Often loses things necessary for tasks or activities at school or at home.
14. Often engages in physically dangerous activities without considering possible consequences (not for the purpose of thrill-seeking), e.g., runs into street without looking.

According to CH.A.D.D., approximately 30% of people with ADD also have learning disabilities. ADD affects approximately 3% to 5% of the school-age population.

Autism

"A developmental disability significantly affecting verbal and non-verbal communication and social interaction, generally evident before age three, that adversely affects educational performance."

According to NICHY, less than 1% of the general population is autistic.

Deaf

"A hearing impairment which is so severe that a child is impaired in processing linguistic information through hearing, with or without amplification, which adversely affects educational performance."

Deaf-Blind

"Simultaneous hearing and visual impairments, the combination of which causes such severe communication and other developmental and educational problems that a child cannot be accommodated in special education programs solely for deaf children or blind children."

Hard of Hearing

"A hearing impairment, whether permanent or fluctuating, which adversely affects a child's educational performance but which is not included under the definition of 'deaf'."

Mentally Retarded

"Significantly subaverage general intellectual functioning existing concurrently with deficits in adaptive behavior and manifested during the developmental period, which adversely affects a child's educational performance."

According to NICHY approximately 1% of the general population has mental retardation.

Multihandicapped

"Simultaneous impairments (such as mentally retarded/blind, mentally retarded/orthopedically impaired, etc.), the combination of which causes such severe educational problems that the child cannot be accommodated in a special education program solely for one of the impairments. The term does not include deaf-blind children."

Orthopedically Impaired

"A severe orthopedic impairment which adversely affects a child's educational performance. The term includes impairments caused by congenital anomaly (e.g. clubfoot, absence of some member, etc.), impairments caused by disease (e.g. poliomyelitis, bone tuberculosis, etc.), and impairments from other causes (e.g., cerebral palsy, amputations, and fractures or burns which cause contractures)."

Other Health Impaired

"Having limited strength, vitality or alertness, due to chronic or acute health problems such as a heart condition, tuberculosis, rheumatic fever, nephritis, asthma, sickle cell anemia, hemophilia, epilepsy, lead poisoning, leukemia, or diabetes, which adversely affects a child's educational performance."

Seriously Emotionally Disturbed

"(I.) A condition exhibiting one or more of the following characteristics over a long period of time and to a marked degree, which adversely affects educational performance: (A) an inability to learn which cannot be explained by intellectual, sensory, or health factors; (B) an inability to build or maintain satisfactory interpersonal relationships with peers and teachers; (C) inappropriate types of behavior or feelings under normal circumstances; (D) a general pervasive mood of unhappiness or depression; or (E) a tendency to develop physical symptoms or fears associated with personal or school problems.

"(II.) The term includes children who are schizophrenic. The term does not include children who are socially maladjusted, unless it is determined that they are seriously emotionally disturbed."

Specific Learning Disability

IDEA Definition: "Specific learning disability means a disorder in one or more of the basic psychological processes involved in understanding or in using language, spoken or written, which may manifest itself in an imperfect ability to listen, think, speak, read, write, spell, or to do mathematical calculations which adversely affects the child's educational performance. The term includes such conditions as perceptual handicaps, brain injury, minimal brain dysfunction, dyslexia, and developmental aphasia. The term does not include children who have learning problems which are primarily the result of visual, hearing or motor handicaps, of mental retardation, of emotional disturbance or of environmental, cultural, or economic disadvantage."

The National Joint Committee on Learning Disabilities Definition: "Learning disabilities is a general term that refers to a heterogeneous group of disorders manifested by significant difficulties in the acquisition and use of listening, speaking, reading, writing, reasoning, or mathematical abilities. These disorders are intrinsic to the individual, presumed to be due to central nervous system dysfunction, and may occur across the life span. Problems in self-regulatory behaviors, social perception, and social interaction may exist with learning disabilities but do not by themselves constitute a learning disability...."

As stated by Dr. Melvin Levine in the Medical Forum, September 1984: "'Learning disability' is the term currently used to describe a handicap that interferes with someone's ability to store, process, or produce information.... Learning disabilities create a gap between a person's true capacity and his day-to-day productivity and performance."

According to the U.S. Department of Health and Human Services: "Dyslexia refers to all reading problems of an undetermined nature - the term should become increasingly narrow in scope until there will not be a need for the term because all causes of reading disorders will have been identified."

According to the Learning Disabilities Association, it is estimated that 12% to 20% of the population may be learning disabled.

Refer to *The Misunderstood Child*, by Larry Silver, M.D., for a good breakdown and recent research findings on learning disabilities and ADD.

Speech Impaired

"A communication disorder such as stuttering, impaired articulation, a language impairment, or a voice impairment, which adversely affects a child's educational performance."

Traumatic Brain Injury

"An injury to the brain caused by an external physical force or by an internal occurrence such as stroke or aneurysm, resulting in total or partial functional disability or psychosocial maladjustment that adversely affects educational performance."

Visually Handicapped

"A visual impairment which, even with correction, adversely affects a child's educational performance. The term includes both partially seeing and blind children."

Appendix B:
Organizations

Information Clearinghouses

Clearinghouse on Disability Information
Office of Special Education and Rehabilitative Services
Room 3132 Switzer Building
330 C Street, SW
Washington, DC 20202   Phone: 202/205-8241

ERIC Clearinghouse on Handicapped and Gifted Children
Council for Exceptional Children (CEC)
1920 Association Drive
Reston, VA 22091–1589   Phone: 800/544-3284

HEATH Resource Center (National Clearinghouse on Postsecondary Education for Individuals with Disabilities)
One Dupont Circle, NW, Suite 800
Washington, DC 20036–1193   Phone: 800/544-3284
                                   (voice and TDD)

National Clearinghouse for Professions in Special Education
1800 Diagonal Road, Suite 320
Alexandria, VA 22314   Phone: 703/519–3800

National Health Information Center
P.O. Box 1133
Washington, DC 20013–1133   Phone: 800/336–4797

National Information Center on Deafness (NICD)
800 Florida Avenue, NE
Washington, DC 20002　　　Phone: 202/651–5051 (voice)
　　　　　　　　　　　　　　　　　202/651–5052 (TDD)

National Information Center for Children and Youth with
Disabilities (NICHY)
P.O. Box 1492
Washington, DC 20013–1492　　　Phone: 800/695–0285

National Maternal and Child Health Clearinghouse
38th and R Streets, NW
Washington, DC 20057　　　Phone: 202/625–8410

National Rehabilitation Information Center (NARIC)
8455 Colesville Road, Suite 935
Sliver Spring, MD 20910–3319　　　Phone: 800/346–2742
　　　　　　　　　　　　　　　　　(voice/TDD)

General

Access to Respite Care and Help (ARCH)
The Chapel Hill Training-Outreach Project
800 Eastowne Drive
Chapel Hill, NC 27514　　　Phone: 919/490–5577
　　　　　　　　　　　　　800/7-RELIEF (773-5433)

American Council of Rural Special Education (ACRES)
Department of Special Education
University of Utah
Milton Bennion Hall
Salt Lake City, UT 84112　　　Phone: 801/581–8442

American Occupational Therapy Association (AOTA)
P.O. Box 1725
1383 Piccard Drive
Rockville, MD 20849–1725　　　Phone: 301/948–9626 (voice)
　　　　　　　　　　　　　　　　301/948–9626 (TDD)

American Physical Therapy Association (APTA)
1111 North Fairfax Street
Alexandria, VA 22314　　　Phone: 703/684–2782

American Speech-Language-Hearing Association (ASHA)
10801 Rockville Pike
Rockville, MD 20852   Phone: 800/638–8255 (voice)
                                         301/897–5700 (voice/TDD)

Association for the Advancement of Rehabilitation Technology (RESNA)
1101 Connecticut Avenue, NW, Suite 700
Washington, DC 20036   Phone: 202/857–1199
                                         (voice/TDD)

Association of Maternal and Child Health Programs
1350 Connecticut Avenue, NW, Suite 803
Washington, DC 20036   Phone: 202/775-0436

Association for the Care of Children's Health (ACCH)
7910 Woodmont Avenue, Suite 300
Bethesda, MD 20814–3015   Phone: 301/654–6549

ARC (formerly Association for Retarded Citizens of the U.S.)
P.O. Box 300649
Arlington, TX 76010   Phone: 817/261–6003 (voice)
                                         817/277–0553 (TDD)

Center for Youth with Disabilities
Adolescent Health Program
University of Minnesota Hospital and Clinic
P.O. Box 721
Harvard Street at East River Road
Minneapolis, MN 55455   Phone: 612/626–2820

Council for Exceptional Children (CEC)
1920 Association Drive
Reston, VA 22091   Phone: 703/620–3660

Family Voices
Box 769
Algodones, NM 87001

Federation of Families for Children's Mental Health
1021 Prince Street
Alexandria, VA 22314-2971   Phone: 703/684-7710

Head Start
Administration on Children, Youth and Families
Office of Human Development Services
U.S. Department of Health and Human Services
P.O. Box 1182
Washington, DC 20013   Phone: 800/245–0572

Independent Living Residential Utilization Project (ILRU)
The Institute for Rehabilitation and Research
2323 South Sheppard, Suite 1000
Houston, TX 77019   Phone: 713/520–0232 (voice)
                      713/520–5136 (TDD)

March of Dimes Birth Defects Foundation
1275 Mamaroneck Avenue
White Plains, NY 10605   Phone: 914/428–7100

*National Center for Education in Maternal and Child
Health*
2000 15th StreetNorth, Suite 701
Arlington, VA 22201-2617   Phone: 703/524-7802

National Easter Seal Society
70 East Lake Street
Chicago, IL 60601   Phone: 800/221–6827 (voice)
                      312/726–4248 (TDD)

National Parent Network on Disabilities (NPND)
1600 Prince Street, Suite 115
Alexandria, VA 22314   Phone: 703/683–NPND (6763)

National Respite Coalition
(a division of the National Respite Network)
4016 Oxford Street
Annandale, VA 22003   Phone: 800/473-1727

Parent-to-Parent Survey Project
Beach Center on Families and Disability
The University of Kansas
Lawrence, KS 66045   Phone: 913/846–7600

Siblings for Significant Change
105 East 22nd Street
New York, NY 10010

Sibling Information Network
Connecticut University Affiliated Program
991 Main Street, Suite 3A
East Hartford, CT 06108   Phone: 203/282–7050

Siblings of Disabled Children
Parents Helping Parents, Inc.
535 Race Street, Suite 220
San Jose, CA 95126

Sick Kids (need) Involved People (SKIP)
990 2nd Avenue, 2nd Floor
New York, NY 10022   Phone: 212/421–9160

Special Olympics
1350 New York Avenue, NW, Suite 500
Washington, DC 20005–4709   Phone: 202/628–3630

Technical Assistance to Parent Programs (TAPP) Network
Central Office
Federation for Children with Special Needs
95 Berkeley Street, Suite 104
Boston, MA 02116   Phone: 800/331–0688

Texas Respite Resource Network (TRRN)
Saint Rosa Children's Hospital
P.O. Box 7330
San Antonio, TX 78207–3198   Phone: 512/228–2794

Trace Research and Development Center on Communication, Control, and Computer Access for Handicapped Individuals
S–151 Waisman Center, 1500 Highland Avenue
University of Wisconsin-Madison
Madison, WI 53705–2280   Phone: 608/262–6966 (voice)
                                 608/262–5408 (TDD)

Disability Specific

American Foundation for the Blind (AFB)
15 West 16th Street
New York, NY 10011   Phone: 800/232–5463 (voice)
                                          212/620–2158 (TDD)

Association for Persons with Severe Handicaps (TASH)
11201 Greenwood Avenue, North
Seattle, WA 98133   Phone: 206/361–8870 (voice)
                                       206/361–0113 (TDD)

Autism Society of America (formerly NSAC)
8601 Georgia Avenue, Suite 503
Sliver Spring, MD 20901   Phone: 301/565–0433

CH.A.D.D. (Children and Adults with Attention Deficit Disorders)
499 Northwest 70th Avenue, Suite 308
Plantation, FL 33317   Phone: 305/587–3700

Epilepsy Foundation of America (EFA)
4351 Garden City Drive, Suite 406
Landover, MD 20785   Phone: 800/332–1000

International Rett Syndrome Association
8511 Rose Marie Drive
Fort Washington, MD 20744   Phone: 301/856-3334

Learning Disability Association of America (LDA)
(formerly ACLD)
4156 Library Road
Pittsburgh, PA 15234   Phone: 412/341–1515

Muscular Dystrophy Association (MDA)
3561 East Sunrise Drive
Tucson, AZ 85718   Phone: 800/223–6666

National Alliance for the Mentally Ill (NAMI)
2101 Wilson Boulevard, Suite 302
Arlington, VA 22201   Phone: 800/950–NAMI (6264)

National Center for Learning Disabilities (NCLD)
381 Park Avenue South, Suite 1420
New York, NY 10016   Phone: 212/687-7211

National Down Syndrome Congress
1800 Dempster Street
Park Ridge, IL 60068–1146   Phone: 800/232–NDSC (6372)

National Down Syndrome Society
666 Broadway
New York, NY 10012   Phone: 800/221–4602

National Head Injury Foundation, Inc.
1140 Connecticut Avenue, NW, Suite 812
Washington, DC 20036   Phone: 202/296–6443

National Spinal Cord Injury Association
600 West Cummings Park, Suite 2000
Woburn, MA 01801   Phone: 800/962–9629

Orton Dyslexia Society
Chester Building #382
8600 LaSalle Road
Baltimore, MD 21204   Phone: 800/222–3123

Skating Association for the Blind and Handicapped
1255 Niagra Falls Boulevard
Buffalo, NY 14226

Spina Bifida Association of America
4590 MacArthur Boulevard, NW, Suite 250
Washington, DC 20007   Phone: 800/621–3141

United Cerebral Palsy Association, Inc.
1522 K Street, NW, Suite 1112
Washington, DC 20005   Phone: 800/872–5827

United States Association of Blind Athletes
33 North Institute
Colorado Springs, CO 80903   Phone: 719/630-0422

Federal Government Agencies

Administration on Developmental Disabilities
U.S. Department of Health and Human Services
Room 329D Humphrey Building
Washington, DC 20201   Phone: 202/673-7678

Architectural and Transportation Barriers
Compliance Board
1331 F Street, NW
Washington, DC 20004   Phone: 800/USA-ABLE (872-2253)
(voice or TDD)

Deafness and Communicative Disorders Branch
U.S. Department of Education
Room 3221 Switzer Building
330 C Street, SW
Washington, DC 20202   Phone: 202/205-9001
202/205-8298 (TDD)

Division of Educational Services
Office of Special Programs
Washington, DC 20202   Phone: 202/554-7699

Equal Employment Opportunity Commission
1801 L Street, NW
Washington, DC 20507   Phone: 202/663-4900
800/800-3302 (TDD)

Federal Communications Commission
1919 M Street, NW
Washington, DC 20554   Phone: 202/632-7260
202/632-6999 (TDD)

Gallaudet University
800 Florida Avenue, NE
Washington, DC 20002   Phone: 202/651-5000

Head Start Bureau
P.O. Box 1182
Washington, DC 20013   Check local phone directory

HEATH Resource Center
One Dupont Circle, Suite 800
Washington, DC 20036-1193   Phone: 800/544-3284

Helen Keller National Center
111 Middle Neck Road
Sands Point, NY 11050   Phone: 516/944-8900
                                     (voice/TDD)

*National Library Services for the Blind and Physically Handicapped**
The Library of Congress
Washington, DC 20542   Phone: 800/424–8567 (voice)
                           800/424–9100 (TDD English)
                           800/345–8901 (TDD Spanish)

National Technical Institute for the Deaf
One Lomb Memorial Drive
Rochester, NY 14623   Phone: 716/475-6400

Office on the Americans with Disabilities Act
Civil Rights Division
U.S. Department of Justice
P.O. Box 66118
Washington, DC 20035–6118   Phone: 202/514-0301
  202/514-0318 (TDD)

Office of Student Financial Assistance
P.O. Box 84
Washington, DC 20044   Phone: 202/274-5061

Small Business Administration
Financial Assistance Division
Handicapped Assistance Loan Program
Suite 8300
409 Third Street, SW
Washington, DC 200416   Phone: 202/205-7701

Social Security Administration
U. S. Department of Health and Human Services
P.O. Box 17743
Baltimore, MD 21235   Phone:800/772-1213

U.S. Department of Transportation
400 Seventh Street, SW
Washington, DC 20590   Phone: 202/366-4000

---

* Offers services to other than blind and physically handicapped.

C Appendix C: Books and Other Publications

The books and other publications included below represent only a fraction of those available. A list of catalog sources and bookstores is provided at the end of this appendix.

Books for Children

Motivation

The Don't-Give-Up Kid and *Learning Differences*, by Jeanne Gehret, published by Verbal Images Press, Fairport, NY.

Keeping A Head in School, by Melvin D. Levine, published by Educators Publishing Service Inc., Cambridge, MA.

The Silver Slippers, by Elizabeth Koda-Callan, published by Workman Publishing, New York, NY.

General

Amelia Bedelia, by Peggy Parish, published by Harper and Row, New York, NY (good examples of what it means to take things literally).

I'm Somebody Too, by Jeanne Gehret, published by Verbal Images Press, Fairport, NY (deals with sibling issues).

Rosey...the Imperfect Angel, by Sandra Lee Peckinpah, published by Scholars Press, Woodland Hills, CA.

Sassafras, by Audrey Penn, published by Child & Family Press, CWLA, Washington, DC (teaches self-esteem).

The Kissing Hand, by Audrey Penn, published by Child & Family Press, CWLA, Washington, DC (helping a child with separation from parents for school or other reasons)

ADD

Eagle Eyes: A Child's Guide to Paying Attention, by Jeanne Gehret, published by Verbal Images Press, Fairport, NY.

Shelley the Hyperactive Turtle, by Deborah Moss, published by Woodbine House, Rockville, MD.

Autism

Russell is Extra Special: A Book About Autism for Children, by Charles Amenta III, M.D., published by Magination Press, New York, NY.

Down Syndrome

Loving Ben, by Elizabeth Laird, published by Delacorte, New York, NY.

Learning Disabilities

What Do You Mean I Have a Learning Disability?, by Kathleen M. Dwyer, published by Walker and Company, New York, NY.

Seizure Disorders

Lee, The Rabbit with Epilepsy, by Deborah Moss, published by Woodbine House, Rockville, MD.

Divorce

The Boys and Girls Book About Divorce, by Richard A. Gardner, M.D., published by Bantam Books, New York, NY.

Videos for Children

It's Just Attention Disorder, by Sam Goldstein and Michael Goldstein, produced by Neurology Learning and Behavior Center, 670 East 3900 South Suite 100, Salt Lake City, UT 84107.

Books about Developmental and Physical Disabilities

Your Child Has A Disability: A Complete Sourcebook of Daily and Medical Care, by Mark L. Batshaw, M.D., published by Little Brown, Boston, MA.

Since Owen: A Parent-to-Parent Guide for Care of the Disabled Child, by Charles R. Callanan, published by John Hopkins University Press, Baltimore, MD.

Steps to Independence: A Skills Training Guide for Parents and Teachers or Children with Special Needs, by Bruce L. Baker and Alan J. Brightman with Jan B. Blacher, Louis J. Heifetz, Stephen P. Hinshaw, and Diane M. Murphy, published by Paul H. Brookes Publishing Company, Baltimore, MD.

Meeting the Challenge of Disability or Chronic Illness: A Family Guide, by Lori A. Goldfarb, Mary Jane Brotherson, Jean Ann Summers, and Ann P. Turnbull, published by Paul H. Brookes Publishing Company, Baltimore, MD.

The Special Child: A Source Book for Parents of Children with Developmental Disabilities, by Siegfred M. Puechel, M.D., James C. Bernier, M.S.W., and Leslie E. Weidenman, Ph.D., published by Paul H. Brookes Publishing Company, Baltimore, MD.

Books and Videos about Specific Disabilities

ADD

A Parent's Guide to Attention Deficit Disorders, by Lisa J. Bain, published by Delta, Philadelphia, PA.

The Hyperactive Child, Adolescent, and Adult: Attention-Deficit Disorder Through the Lifespan, by Paul H. Wender, published by Oxford, New York, NY.

For others, contact ADD Warehouse (800/ADD–WARE (800/233-9273)).

Autism

A Parent's Guide to Autism, by Charles A. Hart, published by Pocket Books Childcare, New York, NY.

Children with Autism: A Parent's Guide, edited by Michael D. Powers, Psy.D., published by Woodbine House, Rockville, MD.

Cerebral Palsy

Children with Cerebral Palsy: A Parent's Guide, edited by Elaine Gualis, published by Woodbine House, Rockville, MD.

Down Syndrome

Babies with Downs Syndrome: A New Parents' Guide, edited by Karen Stray Gundersen, published by Woodbine House, Rockville, MD.

For books on Down syndrome and cerebral palsy, contact Turtle Books (814/696-2920).

Hearing Impairment
Children of Silence, by Kathy Robinson, published by Signet, New York, NY.

Mental Retardation
Retarded Isn't Stupid, Mom!, by Sandra Z. Kaufman, published by Paul H. Brookes Publishing Company, Baltimore, MD.

Learning Disabilities
Fat City, by Richard Lavoie, video available from Riverview School, 551 Route 6A, East Sandwich, MA 02537, 508-888-3699.
The Misunderstood Child, by Larry Silver, M.D. (also information about ADD), Blue Ridge, Summit, PA.
Succeeding Against the Odds, by Sally L. Smith, published by Tarcher, Los Angeles, CA.
Turnabout Children, by Mary MacCracken, published by Signet, Boston, MA.

Seizure Disorders
Children with Epilepsy: A Parent's Guide, by Helen Reisner, published by Woodbine House, Rockville, MD.
Time Out for Families: Epilepsy and Respite Care. Landover, MD: Epilepsy Foundation of America.

Tourette's Syndrome
Children with Tourette's Syndrome: A Parent's Guide, edited by Tracy Hadre, published by Woodbine House, Rockville, MD.

Visual Impairment
Can't Your Child See? A Guide for Parents of Visually Impaired Children, by Eileen P. Scott, James E. Jan, and Roger D. Freeman, published by PRO-ED, Austin, TX.

Books about Transition to Work

Planning for a Job: Tips for Disabled Students, by the President's Committee for Employment of People with Disabilities, Washington, D.C. 20036, 202-653-5044.
Transition from School to Work: New Challenges for Youth with Severe Disabilities, by Paul Wehman, M. Sherril Moon, Jane M. Everson, Wendy Wood, and J. Michael Barcus, published by Paul H. Brookes Publishing Company, Baltimore, MD.
Steps to Independence: A Skills Training Guide for Parents and Teachers of Children with Special Needs, published by Pual H. Brookes Publishing, Baltimore, MD.

General Books

A Difference in the Family: Living with a Disabled Child, by Helen Featherstone, published by Penguin Books, New York, NY.

A Glossary of Special Education, by Phillip Williams, published by Open University Press, Taylor & Francis, Bristol, PA.

A Parents' Guide to Doctors, Disabilities, and the Family, published by NICHY, Washington, DC.

Brothers and Sisters: A Special Part of Exceptional Families, published by Pual H. Brookes Publishing, Baltimore, MD.

Negotiating the Special Education Maze: A Guide for Parents and Teachers, by Winifred Anderson, Stephen Chitwood, and Deidre Hayden, published by Woodbine House, Rockville, MD.

No One to Play With: The Social Side of Learning Disabilities, by Betty B. Osman in association with Henriette Blinder, published by Random House, New York, NY.

Pocket Guide to Federal Help for Individuals with Disabilities, published by the U.S. Department of Education, Office of Special Education and Rehabilitative Services, 400 Maryland Ave., SW, Washington, DC 20202-2524.

Puppetry for Mentally Handicapped People, by Caroline Astell-Burt, published by Souvenir Press, Brookline Books, Cambridge, MA.

Summary of Existing Legislation Affecting People with Disabilities, published by the U.S. Department of Education, Office of Special Education and Rehabilitative Services, 400 Maryland Ave., SW, Washington, DC 20202-2524.

The Working Parents' Guide to Child Care, by Byrne Siegel-Gorelick, Ph.D., published by Little, Brown and Company, Boston, MA.

Behavior Management and Self-Esteem Books and Videos

The Difficult Child, by Stanley Turecki, M.D., with Leslie Tonner, published by Bantam Books, New York, NY.

1-2-3 Magic: Training Your Preschoolers and Preteens to Do What You Want!, by Thomas W. Phelan, a video and book produced by Child Management, available at 1-800-ADD-WARE.

Surviving Your Adolescence, by Thomas W. Phelan, Ph.D., published by Child Management, available at 1-800-ADD-WARE.

Seeds of Self-Esteem, by Robert Brooks, Jane Ward, and Gerard Pottebaum, a video produced by American Guidance Service, 4201 Woodland Rd, Circle Pines, MN 55014-1796.

The Self-Esteem Teacher, by Robert Brooks, Ph.D., published by American Guidance Service, Inc., 4201 Woodland Rd, Circle Pines, MN 55014-1796.

Books about Divorce and Remarriage

The Parents Book About Divorce, by Richard A. Gardner, M.D., published by Bantam Books, New York, NY.

Love and Power in the Step Family: A Practical Guide, by Jamie K. Keshet, published by McGraw-Hill, New York, NY.

Magazines and Newsletters

(Many organizations concerning disabilities also produce newsletters.)

For Sibs Only (ages 4-9); *Sibling Forum* (ages 10+), Family Resource Association, Inc. 35 Haddon Avenue, Shrewsbury, NJ 07701

Sibling Information Network Newsletter, Sibling Information Network, Connecticut University Affiliated Program on Developmental Disabilities, 991 Main Street, Suite 3A, East Hartford, CT 06108.

The Exceptional Parent Magazine, 296 Boylston St, Boston, MA.

Catalogs

(There are also sections on disabilities at Barnes and Noble and B. Dalton bookstores.)

ADD Warehouse (800/ADD-WARE (800/233-9273)).

Childswork/Childsplay catalog (800/962-1141).

Child Welfare League of America (CWLA) catalog (202/638-2952).

Special Needs Selection Catalogue, Charlesbank Bookshops, B.U. Bookstore Mall, 666 Beacon St, Boston, MA 02215.

Woodbine House catalog (800/843-7323).

D Appendix D: Glossary

Advocate: A person who protects the rights of an individual with disabilities, ensuring that the person with disabilities has the services to which he or she is entitled under law.

Assessment: A group of tests and/or observations to determine whether a child qualifies for special education or related services. An assessment is conducted within a discipline area (e.g., physical therapy).

Assistive Technology: Equipment used to assist an individual with disabilities to achieve a greater level of independence.

Audiologist: A specially trained professional who measures a person's ability to hear and understand sounds.

Diagnosis: A medical opinion as to the condition, including cause and prognosis, of a patient.

Educational Objectives: The objectives set forth within the IEP (Individualized Education Plan) that will help the child progress toward his or her educational goals (as stated within the IEP. Objectives should be attainable within a 12-month time period.

Evaluation: A group of assessments that, when combined, provide a comprehensive picture of a child, including his or her strengths and weaknesses. The evaluation helps the Evaluation Team and parents build the IEP.

Evaluation Team: The group of educational professionals who conduct the assessments.

Independent Evaluation: An evaluation conducted outside the school system at the request of parents (subject to appeal by the school system).

IEP (Individualized Education Plan): The 12-month plan for a child with disabilities, containing a comprehensive profile of the child and his or her educational goals and objectives, and specifying the special education or related services to be provided during this period.

Least Restrictive Environment (LRE): A child with disabilities has the right to a free and appropriate education in the least restrictive environment, according to IDEA. The least restrictive environment provision protects a child's right to be educated in such a way that he or she will spend as much time as educationally appropriate in a general education classroom within his or her neighborhood school.

Liaison: A person designated to communicate between the appropriate parties in the child's outside placement and the child's home school district.

Neurologist: A medical doctor specializing in problems of the nervous system.

Nutritionist: A professional specializing in nutrition.

Ophthalmologist: A medical doctor specializing in the eyes and vision.

Optometrist: A professional specializing in vision testing.

Occupational Therapist: A certified specialist who evaluates, creates, and conducts programs to develop an individual's fine motor skills and daily living skills affected by neurological disorders.

Pediatrician: A medical doctor specializing in the treatment of children.

Psychiatrist: A medical doctor specializing in the treatment of mental health problems.

Psychological Test: A test (or series of tests) to evaluate the level of intelligence as well as the learning style of an individual.

Psychologist: A professional specializing in the evaluation of intellectual functioning and emotional development. Psychologists also specialize in the treatment of emotional and behavioral issues.

Physical Therapist: A certified specialist who evaluates, creates, and conducts programs to develop an individual's gross motor skills.

Referral: A formal request to have a child evaluated to determine whether the child is eligible for special education or related services.

Resource Room: A classroom or designated area in which a child may receive special education or related services.

Respite Care: Temporary support to families with members with disabilities. Respite care may come in the form of home care or a temporary residential placement.

Screening: A pre-evaluation process for determining whether a full evaluation is warranted.

Special Education Administrator: The school system administrator responsible for overseeing the special education programs within a school district.

Speech and Language Pathologist: A certified specialist who evaluates, creates, and conducts programs to develop speech and language skills.

Index

THAT'S MY CHILD—Strategies for Parents of Children with Disabilities

by: Lizanne Capper

Date signed out	Name	Date returned